THE PHILOSOPHY OF KARMA

Also by the Same Author

Echoes of Life
Foundations of Living

THE PHILOSOPHY OF KARMA

UNDERSTANDING THE MODERN WORKING CLASS

DR AJAYPAL KALYAN

An imprint of
Srishti Publishers & Distributors

Srishti Publishers & Distributors
A unit of AJR Publishing LLP
212A, Peacock Lane
Shahpur Jat, New Delhi – 110 049

editorial@srishtipublishers.com

First published by Bold,
an imprint of Srishti Publishers & Distributors in 2025

10 9 8 7 6 5 4 3 2 1

Printed and bound in India.

Dedicated to the nation...

Contents

Part 3
Resistance and Revolution

Preface

The history of civilization is often told through the lens of great leaders and empires, but beneath this grand narrative lies the pulse of the working class – the people who toiled, struggled, and sacrificed to build the societies we know today. This book explores the lesser-told story of duty, morality, despotism, the working class's struggle, and revolution, all of which have collectively shaped humanity. The intent is to understand civilization from the lived experiences of ordinary people, not just from the perspective of rulers and conquerors.

Today, as we face economic inequality, authoritarian regimes, and corporate exploitation, the need to examine our moral foundations and the duty of those in power has never been more urgent. This book delves into these concepts to offer insights into the evolution of morality and how it has been manipulated by modern despots, as well as the ongoing struggle of the working class – who have long been the backbone of society yet remain marginalized and exploited. Their resilience, sacrifices, and role in revolutions are brought to the forefront.

Revolution is presented not just as an event but as an ongoing process, with lessons from history applied to today's subtle yet pervasive forms of despotism – economic disparity, authoritarianism, and systemic discrimination. The book aims to foster awareness and empathy by highlighting the stories of the working class, migrants, brain drain and marginalized communities, inspiring readers to question existing structures and take a stand for social causes.

Ultimately, this book is a call for action, urging readers to be active participants in shaping a society that values dignity and equality for all. It emphasizes the importance of collective action in resisting oppression and advocating for change, striving for a future where every individual has the opportunity to live a life of respect and freedom.

Why am I writing this book?

This book is a literary documentation and research of the complex interplay between duty, morality, despotism, and the working-class struggle – forces that have shaped our civilization. I am driven to explore how these themes have influenced societies, both globally and in India, and to honour the stories of ordinary people whose resilience often goes unnoticed. I tried to bring out both prospectives, Indian and global, in one place so that it would be easier to connect them here and in some case studies as well.

The working class has always been the backbone of progress, yet their contributions and sacrifices are frequently overshadowed. This book aims to bring their struggles to the forefront, highlighting their vital role in revolutions and movements throughout history. By giving voice to their experiences, I hope to provide a nuanced understanding of the injustices they face and their ongoing fight for recognition and justice.

I am also compelled to examine the concepts of duty and morality, which are increasingly compromised by the pursuit of power and profit. In a world where despotism persists in subtle yet pervasive forms – authoritarianism, economic inequality, corporate exploitation – it is essential to revisit these principles and challenge the power dynamics at play. This book draws on philosophical perspectives to provide an ethical framework for analyzing these issues and encourages readers to consider their role in confronting modern forms of oppression.

Ultimately, I am writing this book to foster awareness, empathy, and a spirit of collective action. It is a call for social justice, urging readers to reflect on the values that should guide our societies – equality, dignity, and fairness. Through understanding our past and questioning our present, I hope to inspire a future where justice prevails and every individual has the opportunity to thrive.

I invite you to journey with me through the pages of this book to explore the intricacies of power, morality, struggle, and resistance. Together, let us understand how these forces have shaped the world we live in and how they continue to influence our present and future. It is my hope that this book not only informs but also inspires you to reflect on your role in the ongoing quest for a more just and equitable civilization.

PART 1

FOUNDATIONS OF DUTY AND MORALITY

At the heart of human existence lies the enduring question of how we ought to live and what obligations we owe to one another. The foundations of duty and morality have been explored through various philosophical traditions, each offering a unique lens through which to understand the principles that guide moral behaviour. The concept of duty is inseparable from the moral fabric of society, shaping not only our actions but also our understanding of what it means to live ethically. From ancient virtue ethics to modern consequentialist theories, the foundations of duty and morality offer profound insights into the nature of human responsibility.

Duty and morality serve as the compass by which individuals navigate complex social interactions and ethical dilemmas. Throughout history, philosophers have sought to define the essence of moral obligation, leading to diverse theories that continue to shape contemporary moral discourse. In a world governed by diverse cultures and beliefs, the principles of duty and morality remain universal in their quest to define right and wrong. From Kant's deontological imperatives to the consequentialist views of utilitarianism, the exploration of these foundations offers a profound reflection on human conduct and ethical responsibility.

The foundations of duty and morality are rooted in the age-old pursuit of answering the question: What is the right thing

Introduction

At the heart of human existence lies the enduring question of how we ought to live and what obligations we owe to one another. The foundations of duty and morality have been explored through various philosophical traditions, each offering a unique lens through which to understand the principles that guide moral behaviour. The concept of duty is inseparable from the moral fabric of society, shaping not only our actions but also our understanding of what it means to live ethically. From ancient virtue ethics to modern deontological theories, the foundations of duty and morality offer profound insights into the nature of human responsibility.

Duty and morality serve as the compass by which individuals navigate complex social interactions and ethical dilemmas. Throughout history, philosophers have sought to define the essence of moral obligation, leading to diverse theories that continue to shape contemporary moral discourse. In a world governed by diverse cultures and beliefs, the principles of duty and morality remain universal in their quest to define right and wrong. From Kant's deontological imperatives to the consequentialist views of utilitarianism, the exploration of these foundations offers a profound reflection on human conduct and ethical responsibility.

The foundations of duty and morality are rooted in the age-old pursuit of answering the question: '*What is the right thing to do?'* This inquiry has led to the development of key ethical theories that seek to explain not only how we should act but also why we are bound by certain moral obligations. By examining these various perspectives, we gain a deeper understanding of the ethical principles that underlie our choices and actions, providing a framework through which we can strive to lead a morally upright life. Ultimately, the exploration of duty and morality is a reflection of our shared humanity and our desire to create a just and compassionate world.

Duty and Morality

The intersection of duty and morality often presents a complex dilemma. In many situations, the sense of duty aligns with moral principles, guiding individuals to act ethically and responsibly. However, when duty is manipulated by external authorities, it can come into conflict with personal morality. Individuals may find themselves torn between their duty to the state or employer and their own ethical beliefs.

Literature and history are filled with examples of such moral conflict. In George Orwell's *1984*, the protagonist, Winston Smith, grapples with the tension between his duty to the Party and his personal moral revulsion at its totalitarian practices. Similarly, individuals living under oppressive regimes often face difficult choices, weighing their duty to comply with the law against the moral imperative to resist injustice.

The foundations of duty and morality stem from various ethical theories that seek to define how individuals should act, what obligations they owe to others, and what principles underpin moral behaviour. Below are some of the key perspectives on duty and morality:

Deontological Ethics

Deontological ethics, particularly associated with Immanuel Kant, emphasizes that duty is based on adherence to a set of rules or moral laws. According to Kant, morality is grounded in the categorical imperative, which suggests that individuals must act according to principles that can be universally applied. Duty, under this framework, is not about the consequences but about fulfilling obligations because they are inherently right.

Categorical Imperative: 'Act only according to that maxim whereby you can, at the same time, will that it should become a universal law.'

Morality and Autonomy: Kant argues that individuals are morally autonomous and must act out of respect for moral law.

Utilitarianism

Founded by philosophers like Jeremy Bentham and John Stuart Mill, utilitarianism posits that morality is grounded in the principle of utility – the greatest happiness principle. Actions are deemed moral if they maximize pleasure or happiness and minimize pain or suffering for the greatest number of people.

Consequentialism: The morality of an action is judged solely by its consequences.

Hedonic Calculus: Bentham proposed that we can measure the moral worth of an action by calculating the amount of pleasure or pain it will produce.

Virtue Ethics

Rooted in the philosophy of Aristotle, virtue ethics emphasizes the development of moral character and virtues like courage, honesty, and wisdom. According to this view, morality is about being the right kind of person and performing actions that stem from good character traits.

Eudaimonia (Flourishing): The ultimate goal of life is to achieve eudaimonia, often translated as 'flourishing' or 'happiness', through living a virtuous life.

Moral Duty in Virtue Ethics: Morality is about nurturing virtues that contribute to personal and societal well-being.

Social Contract Theory

Thinkers like Thomas Hobbes, John Locke, and Jean-Jacques Rousseau argue that moral and political duties arise from a social contract, an implicit agreement among individuals to form a society. In this view, individuals consent to abide by certain rules and obligations in exchange for the benefits of social cooperation.

State of Nature: Hobbes described the state of nature as a lawless, violent condition, and the social contract emerges as a necessity for peace and order.

Moral Duty: Moral duties are shaped by the need to maintain a stable, just society.

Ethical Relativism

Ethical relativism suggests that morality is not absolute but is relative to the cultural or societal context. Different cultures have different moral codes, and there is no objective standard by which one can judge another culture's ethics.

Cultural Relativism: Morality is a product of cultural norms and practices, meaning what is considered moral in one society may not be in another.

Criticism: One challenge to ethical relativism is that it may allow for practices that violate fundamental human rights.

Divine Command Theory

This theory posits that morality is derived from the commands of a divine being. According to this view, moral obligations are grounded in religious faith, and actions are morally right if they align with divine law.

Moral Duty: Human beings must act in accordance with God's will, and moral truths are revealed through religious teachings.

Criticism: The theory faces challenges like the Euthyphro dilemma – whether something is good because God commands it or if God commands it because it is good.

So, the foundations of duty and morality are diverse, ranging from rule-based obligations (deontology) to consequence-based ethics (utilitarianism) and the cultivation of virtues (virtue ethics). Each perspective offers a unique understanding of what it means to be moral and how duties to others are defined and grounded in different philosophical, cultural, and theological traditions. Ultimately, understanding these perspectives allows individuals to navigate the complexities of moral decision-making and align their actions with their ethical values.

Chapter 1
Duty in the Context of Society

Duty is a concept deeply ingrained in human societies, embodying the moral or legal obligations that individuals have towards others or their communities. Philosophers such as Immanuel Kant have argued that duty is the cornerstone of ethical behaviour, emphasizing that actions should be guided by a sense of duty rather than by personal desires or outcomes. In many cultures, duty is interwoven with notions of honour, responsibility, and societal roles, dictating how individuals ought to conduct themselves.

Throughout history, the perception of duty has been shaped by various forces, including religious doctrines, cultural norms, and political ideologies. In ancient societies, duty was often seen as a divine command, with individuals bound to fulfil their roles within a cosmically ordained order. In contrast, modern secular societies may derive duty from social contracts or legal frameworks, emphasizing the importance of contributing to the common good. The concept of duty has thus evolved, but its core idea of binding individuals to a higher cause remains constant.

Duty and the Working Class

The working class has historically been conditioned to perceive duty in terms of labour and productivity. In capitalist societies, the idea of duty is often tied to the notion of hard work, where individuals are expected to toil diligently for the benefit of the economy and, by extension, the nation. This duty to work is reinforced through cultural narratives that valorize self-sacrifice and the pursuit of upward mobility, often ignoring the systemic inequalities that limit opportunities for the working class.

Workers are portrayed as the backbone of the nation, and in totalitarian states, this sense of duty is taken to an extreme. Their labour is exalted as a patriotic duty. However, this glorification of work masks the exploitation and dehumanization of workers, who are denied basic rights and subjected to harsh conditions in the name of national progress. The duty to work becomes a means of suppressing dissent, as any resistance to exploitation is framed as a betrayal of the collective good.

Cultural Perceptions of Duty

Cultural context plays a significant role in shaping perceptions of duty. In collectivist cultures, such as those in many Asian societies, duty is often seen as a communal responsibility, emphasizing harmony, obedience, and loyalty to the group. In these societies, individuals are expected to fulfil their roles within the family, community, and nation, often subordinating personal desires to the needs of the collective.

In contrast, individualistic cultures, particularly in the West, tend to prioritize personal autonomy and self-fulfilment. While duty is still recognized, it is often framed in terms of personal responsibility rather than collective obligation. This can lead to a more flexible interpretation of duty, where individuals are encouraged to pursue their own paths while contributing to society in ways that align with their personal values.

Concept of Duty in Various Political and Social Systems

The concept of duty is a fundamental aspect of human societies, influencing how individuals perceive their roles and responsibilities within a community. Duty is often shaped by the political and social systems in which people live, and it plays a key role in maintaining social order, cohesion, and governance. The interpretation and enforcement of duty can vary significantly across different systems, such as democratic societies and totalitarian regimes. Understanding these variations provides insight into how different systems operate and the impact they have on individual and collective behaviour.

Duty in Democratic Societies

Democratic societies are characterized by their emphasis on individual rights, freedoms, and the active participation of citizens in governance. In such societies, the concept of duty is multifaceted, encompassing civic responsibility, the protection of individual and collective rights, and the moral obligation to contribute to the common good.

Civic Duty and Political Participation: One of the fundamental aspects of duty in democratic societies is the concept of civic duty. Civic duty refers to the responsibilities of citizens to engage in activities that support the functioning and integrity of the democratic process. This includes voting, participating in public debate, serving on juries, and being informed about political and social issues.

Voting is often considered the most basic and crucial expression of civic duty in a democracy. It is through the act of voting that citizens exercise their sovereignty, choosing representatives who will make decisions on their behalf.

By participating in elections, individuals contribute to the legitimacy and accountability of the government. The duty to vote is not just about casting a ballot; it also involves making informed choices, understanding the policies and positions of candidates, and considering the broader impact of electoral outcomes on society.

Beyond voting, democratic societies encourage active participation in various forms of civic engagement. This can include attending town hall meetings, engaging in peaceful protest, volunteering for community service, and advocating for causes that promote social justice and equality. These activities reflect the idea that democracy is not merely a system of government but a way of life that requires ongoing involvement and commitment from its citizens.

Duty to uphold Rights and Freedom: In democracies, there is a reciprocal relationship between rights and duties. While individuals are granted certain rights and freedoms, they also have a duty to respect the rights and freedoms of others. This involves adhering to the rule of law, which is a fundamental principle of democratic governance. The rule of law ensures that laws are applied equally and fairly, protecting individuals from arbitrary power and abuse.

The duty to uphold rights and freedoms extends to various aspects of social life. For example, individuals have a duty to respect others' freedom of speech, even if they disagree with the views being expressed. This tolerance is essential for maintaining a healthy democratic discourse where diverse opinions can be debated and considered. Similarly, individuals have a duty to respect the right to peaceful assembly, the right to privacy, and the right to due process under the law.

The state, in turn, has a duty to protect the rights and freedoms of its citizens. This includes ensuring that individuals have access to essential services such as education, healthcare, and security, as well as safeguarding civil liberties such as freedom of speech, assembly, and the press. The state is also responsible for providing mechanisms for individuals to seek redress and justice in cases where their rights are violated. This reciprocal duty between citizens and the state is central to the functioning of a democratic society, where power is derived from the consent of the governed.

Social and Ethical Duty: In addition to civic and legal duties, democratic societies place a strong emphasis on social and ethical duty. This aspect of duty involves acting in ways that promote the common good and contribute to the well-being of the community. It includes showing respect and tolerance for diversity, engaging in ethical behaviour, and taking responsibility for one's actions.

Social and ethical duty is reflected in the expectation that individuals will contribute positively to society, whether through their work, family life, or community involvement. This can involve volunteering for charitable causes, participating in local initiatives, or simply being a good neighbour. The emphasis on social duty in democracies fosters a sense of collective responsibility, where individuals are encouraged to look beyond their own interests and consider the impact of their actions on others.

The moral dimension of duty in democratic societies also extends to issues such as social justice and environmental stewardship. Citizens are encouraged to advocate for policies and practices that promote equality, protect the vulnerable, and preserve the environment for future generations. This broader conception of duty reflects the idea that individuals have a role to play in shaping a just and sustainable society.

Balancing Individual Rights and Collective Responsibility: A key challenge in democratic societies is balancing individual rights with collective responsibility. Democracies value personal freedom and autonomy, but they also recognize that individuals have a duty to contribute to the collective well-being. This balance is evident in debates over issues such as taxation, public health, and environmental regulation, where the rights of individuals must be weighed against the needs of the community.

For example, paying taxes is considered a civic duty in democracies, as it provides the resources necessary for the government to function and deliver public services. However, the level and use of taxation can be a contentious issue, with differing views on how much individuals should be required to contribute and how public funds should be allocated. Similarly, public health measures, such as vaccination and social distancing during a pandemic, involve a trade-off between individual freedoms and the duty to protect public health.

In democratic societies, the concept of duty is thus inherently dynamic and subject to ongoing negotiation. It requires individuals to be actively engaged in the democratic process, not only to assert their rights but also to fulfil their responsibilities to others.

Duty in Totalitarian Regimes

In stark contrast to democratic societies, totalitarian regimes impose a very different concept of duty on individuals.

Totalitarianism is characterized by the absolute authority of the state, which seeks to control all aspects of public and private life. In such systems, the concept of duty is often manipulated to serve the interests of the ruling party or leader, with little regard for individual rights or freedoms.

Duty to the State and Leader: In totalitarian regimes, the primary duty of individuals is to the state and its leader. This duty is often framed in terms of loyalty, obedience, and sacrifice. Citizens are expected to place the interests of the state above their own, demonstrating unwavering support for the ruling ideology and leadership. The state demands total allegiance, and any deviation from this duty is considered an act of treason or subversion.

Totalitarian regimes employ propaganda, education, and surveillance to instil a sense of duty in their citizens. From an early age, individuals are indoctrinated to believe that their highest duty is to serve the state, often through compulsory activities such as military service, participation in state-sponsored organizations, or involvement in mass rallies and demonstrations. The leader is often elevated to a near-divine status, and expressions of loyalty to the leader become synonymous with fulfilling one's duty to the state.

Suppression of Individual Rights: In totalitarian systems, the concept of duty is used to justify the suppression of individual rights and freedoms. The state imposes strict controls on speech, assembly, and association, and any form of dissent is punished severely. Citizens are expected to conform to the state's directives without question, and there is little room for personal autonomy or moral agency.

The state's demands on individuals extend into every aspect of life, including personal beliefs, cultural practices, and family relationships. The duty to the state takes precedence over all other loyalties, including those to family, community, or religious institutions. In some cases, totalitarian regimes actively encourage individuals to report on the activities of their neighbours, colleagues, or even family members, reinforcing the notion that loyalty to the state supersedes all other forms of duty.

The suppression of individual rights in totalitarian regimes is often justified by the state's claim to represent the collective will or destiny of the nation. The state's authority is seen as absolute, and individuals are expected to subordinate their own desires and interests to the goals of the state. This creates an environment where individuals are compelled to act out of fear and self-preservation rather than a genuine sense of duty or commitment to the common good.

The Role of Fear and Coercion: The concept of duty in totalitarian regimes is often enforced through fear and coercion. The state uses mechanisms of control such as secret police, surveillance, and punitive measures to ensure compliance. The duty to obey is not motivated by a sense of civic responsibility or moral conviction but rather by the fear of retribution. This creates an environment where individuals are compelled to act out of self-preservation rather than genuine commitment to the state's ideals.

In George Orwell's *1984*, the totalitarian regime of Oceania exemplifies this use of fear and coercion to enforce duty. The state's surveillance apparatus, the Thought Police, and the threat of punishment for 'thoughtcrime' serve to instil fear in the populace, compelling them to show outward loyalty and obedience to Big Brother. In such an environment, the concept of duty is reduced to a form of forced compliance, stripped of any ethical significance.

The use of fear and coercion undermines the ethical foundations of duty, reducing it to a tool of control rather than a moral obligation. In totalitarian regimes, the individual's sense of duty is not a freely chosen commitment but a forced compliance with the state's demands. This perversion of duty strips it of its ethical significance and turns it into an instrument of oppression.

Manipulation of Moral Duty: Totalitarian regimes often manipulate the concept of moral duty to align it with the interests of the state. They present their ideology as a moral imperative, framing the duty to the state as a righteous and noble cause. This manipulation of moral duty serves to justify the state's actions and policies, even when they involve the suppression of rights, violence, or injustice.

For instance, in Maoist China, the duty to participate in the Cultural Revolution was framed as a moral obligation to purify society and eliminate counter-revolutionary elements. Individuals were encouraged to denounce those who were perceived as enemies of the state, including family members and colleagues. The state's ideology was presented as the ultimate moral authority, and any deviation from it was seen as a betrayal of the collective good.

This manipulation of moral duty serves to create a sense of moral absolutism, where the state's ideology is equated with moral truth. Individuals are conditioned to view their duty to the state as the highest moral obligation and any dissent is seen as a moral failing. This creates a society where ethical considerations are subsumed under the state's demands, and individuals are denied the moral agency to question or challenge the state's authority.

Comparative Analysis: Democratic versus Totalitarian Duty

The concept of duty in democratic societies is rooted in the idea of mutual respect, individual rights, and social responsibility. It emphasizes the importance of active citizenship, ethical behaviour, and the protection of individual freedoms. Duty in democracies is seen as a voluntary and reciprocal relationship between the individual and the state, where citizens contribute to the common good while enjoying the protection of their rights.

In contrast, duty in totalitarian regimes is imposed and absolute, with the state demanding complete loyalty and obedience from its citizens. It is a duty that is enforced through coercion and fear, with little regard for individual autonomy or moral agency. The state's interests take precedence over individual rights, and the concept of duty is manipulated to justify the suppression of dissent and the control of every aspect of life.

While democratic societies view duty as a means of promoting civic engagement and the common good, totalitarian regimes use the concept of duty as a tool of control and oppression. This fundamental difference highlights the divergent ways in which political and social systems shape the understanding and practice of duty, with profound implications for individual and collective life.

The concept of duty varies significantly across different political and social systems, reflecting the underlying values and power structures of each system. In democratic societies, duty is associated with civic responsibility, individual rights, and ethical behaviour. It is a reciprocal relationship that encourages active participation in the democratic process and respect for the rights of others. In totalitarian regimes, duty is imposed as an absolute obligation to the state and its leader, enforced through coercion and fear.

Understanding these differences provides insight into the ways in which political systems shape the behaviour and values of individuals, as well as the impact of these systems on the nature of duty itself. The contrast between democratic and totalitarian concepts of duty underscores the importance of political and social structures in defining the roles and responsibilities of individuals within society. It also highlights the need for vigilance in protecting the principles of freedom, justice, and human dignity, which form the ethical foundation of duty in a truly democratic society.

Concept of Duty in Various Political and Social Systems in the Indian Context

The concept of duty has been an integral part of Indian society and culture for millennia. Rooted in ancient philosophical and religious texts, duty, or 'dharma', has guided individual behaviour, social norms, and governance in India. The notion of duty in India has evolved over time and has been influenced by historical events, cultural transformations, and political changes. This evolution is particularly evident when comparing the ideals of duty in democratic and totalitarian contexts within India.

Duty in Democratic India

India is the world's largest democracy, with a complex socio-political landscape shaped by its diverse cultural, linguistic, and religious fabric. The Indian Constitution, adopted in 1950, enshrines the principles of democracy, secularism, and individual rights, laying the foundation for the concept of duty in modern India.

Civic Duty and Political Participation

In democratic India, civic duty is central to the functioning of the state and society. The Indian Constitution grants citizens the right to vote, freedom of speech, and the right to equality, among others. Alongside these rights, it emphasizes the duties of citizens, which are outlined in the Constitution's 'Fundamental Duties' (Article 51A). These duties include respecting the national symbols, cherishing the nation's heritage, protecting the environment, and promoting harmony among citizens.

Voting is a key aspect of civic duty in India, where citizens have the responsibility to participate in the electoral process. Despite challenges such as illiteracy, poverty, and political corruption, India has witnessed a strong tradition of electoral participation. High voter turnouts, even in the face of social and economic challenges, reflect a widespread acknowledgement of the importance of this civic duty. This participation is seen as a means of holding elected representatives accountable and ensuring that the government remains responsive to the needs and aspirations of the people.

Moreover, political participation in India extends beyond voting. Citizens engage in various forms of civic activism, from participating in public protests to joining non-governmental organizations (NGOs) and community initiatives. The Indian democratic ethos encourages citizens to voice their opinions, advocate for social change, and contribute to the nation's development. This active engagement reflects the idea that democracy in India is not just about casting a vote but about being an informed and involved member of society.

Duty to uphold Rights and Social Justice

In India, the duty to uphold rights and social justice is deeply intertwined with the country's democratic values. The Indian Constitution guarantees fundamental rights to all citizens, including the right to equality, freedom of speech and expression, and the right to education. Alongside these rights, there is a collective duty to ensure that these rights are upheld and that justice is accessible to all.

India's struggle for independence, led by figures like Mahatma Gandhi and Jawaharlal Nehru, was not only a fight for political freedom but also for social justice and equality. This legacy has influenced the nation's understanding of duty, emphasizing the need to address social inequalities and promote inclusivity. For instance, affirmative action policies, such as reservations in education and employment for Scheduled Castes, Scheduled Tribes, and Other Backward Classes, reflect a societal duty to redress historical injustices and provide equal opportunities.

Moreover, the duty to uphold social justice extends to addressing issues such as gender inequality, caste discrimination, and religious intolerance. Civil society organizations, activists, and ordinary citizens play a crucial role in advocating for the rights of marginalized groups and working towards a more just and equitable society. This commitment to social justice is seen as an essential component of India's democratic duty, where individuals and institutions alike are expected to contribute to the common good.

Social and Ethical Duty in Indian Society

The concept of duty in India is also deeply rooted in the cultural and ethical framework of 'dharma'. Derived from ancient Hindu philosophy, dharma refers to the moral and ethical duties that guide an individual's conduct. In the Indian context, dharma extends beyond religious connotations and encompasses a broad range of social and ethical responsibilities.

In democratic India, dharma can be seen in the emphasis on communal harmony, respect for diversity, and the promotion of social welfare. The country's cultural diversity, with its multitude of religions, languages, and traditions, underscores the importance of mutual respect and tolerance. This respect for diversity is not just a legal obligation but a moral duty that reflects the ethos of Indian society.

Ethical duty in India also involves contributing to the welfare of the community. This is evident in practices such as 'seva' (selfless service) and 'daan' (charitable giving), which are encouraged across various religious and cultural traditions. These practices emphasize the moral responsibility of individuals to help those in need, support social causes, and contribute to the well-being of society.

Duty in Totalitarian contexts in India

While India is primarily a democratic nation, there have been moments in its history where totalitarian tendencies have emerged, challenging the democratic ideals of duty and individual rights. The most prominent example of this is the Emergency period (1975-77), when then-Prime Minister Indira Gandhi imposed a state of emergency, curtailing civil liberties and centralizing power.

The Emergency Period: A Case of Totalitarian Duty

During the Emergency, the concept of duty in India took on a totalitarian character. The government imposed strict censorship, suspended democratic processes, and detained political opponents without trial. The state demanded absolute loyalty and compliance from citizens, using coercion and fear to enforce its authority. The duty of citizens was redefined as unquestioning obedience to the government, and any form of dissent was labelled as anti-national or subversive.

The Emergency Period saw the suppression of fundamental rights, including freedom of speech, freedom of the press, and the right to assemble. The duty to uphold these rights, which is central to a democratic society, was overridden by the state's emphasis on maintaining order and national security. The state's actions were justified in the name of preserving the nation's unity and stability, reflecting a totalitarian approach to duty where the ends were seen to justify the means.

This period serves as a stark reminder of how the concept of duty can be manipulated to serve the interests of those in power at the expense of individual rights and democratic principles. It highlights the dangers of totalitarianism and the importance of safeguarding democratic values and the rule of law.

Manipulation of Moral Duty

Totalitarian tendencies in India have also been observed in instances where moral duty is manipulated for political ends. For example, in times of communal tension or conflict, political actors may invoke notions of duty to the community or nation to justify exclusionary or oppressive practices. This manipulation of moral duty can lead to the marginalization of certain groups and the erosion of social cohesion.

The invocation of duty in such contexts often involves the promotion of a singular national or cultural identity to which all citizens are expected to conform. This undermines the pluralistic and inclusive nature of Indian society, where diversity is seen as a source of strength. The use of moral duty to justify discrimination or violence against minority groups poses a serious challenge to the democratic ideals of equaiity, justice, and individual rights.

Comparative Analysis: Democratic and Totalitarian Duty in India

The concept of duty in democratic India is grounded in the principles of individual rights, social justice, and active citizenship. It emphasizes the importance of civic participation, the protection of fundamental rights, and the promotion of the common good. In contrast, the instances of totalitarian duty in India's history, such as during the Emergency, reflect an authoritarian approach where duty is imposed by the state, and individual rights are subordinated to the interests of those in power.

The democratic duty in India involves a dynamic and reciprocal relationship between the state and citizens. It requires individuals to actively engage in the democratic process, contribute to social welfare, and respect the rights of others. This concept of duty is rooted in the idea of 'swaraj' (self-rule), as envisioned by Mahatma Gandhi, where self-discipline and responsibility are essential for the functioning of a free and just society.

On the other hand, totalitarian duty in the Indian context is characterized by the centralization of power, the suppression of dissent, and the imposition of a singular notion of loyalty to the state. It reflects a top-down approach where duty is enforced through coercion and propaganda rather than being a freely chosen commitment to democratic ideals.

The concept of duty in India is shaped by its rich cultural heritage, democratic values, and historical experiences. In a democratic context, duty encompasses civic responsibility, the protection of rights, and ethical conduct, reflecting the principles of equality, justice, and active participation. This democratic duty is integral to the functioning of Indian society, where individuals are encouraged to contribute to the common good while respecting the diversity and rights of others.

However, the Indian experience also includes moments where totalitarian tendencies have challenged these democratic ideals. The Emergency period serves as a stark reminder of how duty can be manipulated to serve the interests of those in power at the expense of individual freedoms and democratic principles. This contrast underscores the importance of vigilance in protecting the democratic ethos and ensuring that the concept of duty remains aligned with the values of freedom, justice, and human dignity.

In contemporary India, the ongoing challenge is to navigate the complexities of duty in a way that upholds the democratic ideals enshrined in the Constitution while addressing the diverse needs and aspirations of its people. The balance between individual rights and collective responsibility, between cultural heritage and social progress, is central to this endeavour. As India continues to evolve, the concept of duty will remain a crucial aspect of its political and social fabric, shaping the nation's journey toward a more just and inclusive society.

Individual versus Collective Duty

The tension between individual and collective duty is a fundamental theme in the moral and ethical discourse of societies throughout history. It reflects the ongoing negotiation between personal autonomy and social responsibility, a balance that shapes the functioning of communities, governments, and institutions. Individual duty emphasizes the responsibilities and obligations that a person owes to themselves, such as personal development, integrity, and the pursuit of happiness. In contrast, collective duty focuses on the responsibilities that individuals have toward the larger community, encompassing ideas of social welfare, public good, and mutual support. This interplay between individual and collective duty is complex, and understanding it requires exploring its philosophical, cultural, and practical dimensions.

The Philosophical Foundations of Individual and Collective Duty

Philosophical perspectives on duty have long grappled with the relationship between the individual and the collective. Western philosophy, from the Ancient Greeks to modern thinkers, has offered varying interpretations of this relationship. In Eastern traditions, particularly within Indian and Chinese philosophies, the balance between individual and collective duties is also a central theme.

Western Perspectives

In Western philosophy, Immanuel Kant's deontological ethics emphasize the importance of individual duty grounded in universal moral laws. According to Kant, individuals have a duty to act according to principles that can be universally applied, irrespective of the consequences. This notion of duty is inherently individualistic, as it places the moral responsibility on the individual to determine and follow a rational moral law. For Kant, the concept of the 'categorical imperative' serves as a guide for individuals to act in ways that respect the dignity and autonomy of others, effectively linking individual duty to the broader ethical imperative of treating others as ends in themselves, not merely as means.

John Stuart Mill's utilitarianism, on the other hand, introduces a more collective approach to duty. Mill argues that the rightness of an action is determined by its ability to promote the greatest happiness for the greatest number. This perspective shifts the focus from individual moral laws to the collective consequences of actions. In this view, individuals have a duty to consider the impact of their actions on the overall well-being of society, suggesting that collective duty takes precedence when it leads to the greater good.

These two philosophical approaches – Kantian deontology and Mill's utilitarianism – highlight the tension between individual and collective duty. Kant emphasizes the primacy of individual moral responsibility, while Mill advocates for a more collective approach, where the outcomes of actions and their effects on the broader community are paramount.

Eastern Perspectives

Eastern philosophies offer a different lens through which to view the relationship between individual and collective duty. In Indian philosophy, the concept of 'Duty' is central. Duty refers to the moral and ethical duties that are specific to an individual's role, stage of life, and circumstances. It encompasses both individual and collective responsibilities, suggesting that individuals must fulfil their personal duties in a way that contributes to the harmony and order of the community.

In Confucianism, the emphasis is on relational duties and the roles individuals play within a hierarchical social order. The focus is on collective harmony and the fulfilment of duties within family and society. Individual duties are seen as integral to maintaining social order and collective well-being. The Confucian ideal of 'ren' (benevolence) suggests that one's duty extends beyond oneself to include others, fostering a sense of interconnectedness and mutual obligation.

Individual Duty: Autonomy and Moral Responsibility

Individual duty centres on the idea of personal responsibility, autonomy, and the pursuit of one's moral principles. It emphasizes the importance of self-governance and the capacity to make ethical decisions independently of external pressures. This form of duty is often associated with concepts such as integrity, self-discipline, and the development of personal virtues.

Personal Autonomy

Personal autonomy is a key aspect of individual duty. It involves the ability to make choices and take actions based on one's values, beliefs, and moral reasoning. In societies that value individualism, autonomy is often regarded as a fundamental right, where individuals are free to pursue their own paths and define their own sense of duty. This autonomy is not only about freedom from external control but also about the ability to act in accordance with one's moral convictions.

The notion of individual duty encompasses various aspects of personal life, such as the duty to oneself to achieve self-improvement, to act with integrity, and to pursue one's happiness. For instance, an individual may feel a duty to pursue education, develop their talents, and seek personal fulfilment. This pursuit is seen as a way of contributing to society, as individuals who achieve their potential can use their abilities to benefit others.

Moral Responsibility

Individual duty also involves moral responsibility, which is the obligation to act in accordance with one's ethical beliefs and principles. This responsibility requires individuals to reflect on their actions, consider the moral implications, and take ownership of the consequences. It implies that individuals are accountable for their choices and must strive to act in ways that align with their moral values.

Moral responsibility can sometimes come into conflict with collective norms or expectations. For example, a whistleblower who exposes unethical practices within an organization may be acting out of a sense of individual moral duty, even if their actions go against the collective interests of their employer. In such cases, the individual's duty to uphold their ethical principles takes precedence over collective loyalty, highlighting the complex interplay between personal and social obligations.

Collective Duty: Social Responsibility and the Common Good

Collective duty refers to the responsibilities individuals have toward the larger community, society, or even humanity as a whole. It emphasizes the idea that individuals are part of a broader social fabric and that their actions have implications for others. Collective duty involves contributing to the common good, supporting social welfare, and working towards the betterment of society.

Social Responsibility

Social responsibility is a key component of collective duty. It involves acting in ways that benefit society and contribute to the well-being of others. This includes fulfilling roles and obligations that support social structures, such as obeying laws, paying taxes, and participating in community service. Social responsibility also extends to advocating for social justice, environmental sustainability, and the protection of human rights.

In many cultures, social responsibility is seen as a moral imperative that transcends individual interests. For example, in the context of environmental stewardship, individuals have a collective duty to protect the planet for future generations. This duty involves making choices that reduce harm to the environment, such as conserving resources, reducing waste, and supporting sustainable practices. The idea is that individuals must consider the broader impact of their actions on society and the environment, recognizing that their responsibilities extend beyond their own immediate needs and desires.

The Common Good

The concept of the common good is central to collective duty. It refers to the idea that individuals have a shared responsibility to promote the overall welfare of society. The common good encompasses the well-being of all members of the community, including access to basic needs such as healthcare, education, and security. In this context, collective duty involves working towards conditions that allow everyone to thrive and achieve their potential.

Collective duty is often institutionalized through laws, policies, and social norms that define the responsibilities of individuals and groups. For instance, in democratic societies, collective duty is reflected in civic duties such as voting, jury service, and community involvement. These duties are seen as essential for maintaining a functioning and equitable society where individuals contribute to the decision-making processes and the maintenance of social order.

In times of crisis, such as natural disasters or pandemics, the notion of collective duty becomes particularly salient. Individuals are called upon to act in ways that support the greater good, such as following public health guidelines, supporting relief efforts, and showing solidarity with those affected. The emphasis on collective duty in such situations underscores the importance of mutual support and cooperation in overcoming challenges and building resilience within communities.

The Balance between Individual and Collective Duty

The relationship between individual and collective duty is not one of opposition but of balance. While individual duty emphasizes personal autonomy and moral responsibility, collective duty focuses on social responsibility and the common good. The challenge lies in finding a balance that allows individuals to fulfil their personal obligations while contributing to the well-being of society.

The Role of Society and Institutions

Societies and institutions play a crucial role in mediating the balance between individual and collective duty. Laws, cultural norms, and social institutions establish frameworks that guide behaviour and define the boundaries of individual and collective responsibilities. For example, legal systems establish individual rights and freedoms while also setting forth collective duties, such as obeying laws and paying taxes. Educational institutions, religious organizations, and community groups also shape the understanding of duty by teaching values, promoting social norms, and encouraging civic engagement.

In democratic societies, the balance between individual and collective duty is negotiated through public discourse, political participation, and the rule of law. Citizens have the opportunity to engage in debates about the distribution of responsibilities, the allocation of resources, and the definition of the common good. This process allows for a dynamic interplay between individual and collective interests, where different perspectives are considered and compromises are made.

Conflicts and Resolutions

Conflicts between individual and collective duty can arise in various contexts, such as when individual freedoms are perceived to be in tension with social norms or when personal interests conflict with the needs of the community. These conflicts require careful consideration and often involve ethical dilemmas.

For instance, in the context of public health, individual freedoms such as the right to personal autonomy and privacy may come into conflict with the collective duty to protect public health. Vaccination mandates, quarantine measures, and health surveillance are examples of situations where the balance between individual rights and collective responsibilities must be negotiated. The resolution of such conflicts often involves finding a compromise that respects individual autonomy while ensuring the safety and well-being of the broader community.

Similarly, in issues of social justice, individuals may face conflicts between their personal interests and the collective duty to address inequality and injustice. For example, addressing systemic discrimination may require individuals and institutions to make sacrifices or changes that challenge the status quo. The pursuit of the common good in such cases involves a willingness to consider the impact of one's actions on others and to take collective action to create a more just and equitable society.

The interplay between individual and collective duty is a central theme in ethical and social discourse. Individual duty emphasizes personal autonomy, moral responsibility, and the pursuit of one's values and principles. Collective duty, on the other hand, focuses on social responsibility, the common good, and the welfare of the broader community. Both aspects of duty are essential for the functioning of society, as they provide the moral and ethical foundation for individual behaviour and social cooperation.

Finding the balance between individual and collective duty is an ongoing process that involves negotiation, compromise, and reflection. It requires individuals to consider the broader impact of their actions on society while also respecting personal autonomy and moral integrity. Societies and institutions play a key role in shaping this balance, providing the frameworks and norms that guide behaviour and define the boundaries of individual and collective responsibilities.

Ultimately, the relationship between individual and collective duty is one of interdependence. Individuals contribute to the collective good through their actions, while the collective provides the conditions that enable individuals to flourish. This mutual relationship underscores the importance of both personal and social responsibilities in creating a just, harmonious, and sustainable society.

Duty in Military Contexts

The Nature of Duty in the Military

Duty in the military context is characterized by a profound sense of responsibility, discipline, and commitment to a cause greater than oneself. The military's primary objective is to protect the nation, maintain peace, and uphold national security. As such, the concept of duty in this setting involves a high level of sacrifice, loyalty, and adherence to a strict code of conduct. Military personnel are expected to place the mission and the well-being of their unit above their personal interests, even at the risk of their own lives.

Obedience and Hierarchical Structure

One of the core aspects of military duty is obedience to authority. The military operates within a hierarchical structure where orders are given and expected to be followed without question. This structure is essential for maintaining discipline and ensuring that decisions can be executed swiftly and effectively, especially in high-stress situations. The duty to obey orders is fundamental to the military ethos, as it ensures unity of action and cohesion within the ranks.

However, this duty to obey is not absolute. Military personnel are also taught the importance of moral and legal judgment. They are trained to recognize when an order is unlawful or goes against the principles of military ethics. In such cases, they have a duty to refuse to follow orders that would lead to unlawful actions or violations of human rights. This creates a complex dynamic where the duty to obey must be balanced with the duty to act ethically and in accordance with international laws and conventions.

Sacrifice and Commitment

The military concept of duty often involves a willingness to make personal sacrifices for the greater good. This can include enduring harsh conditions, being separated from family and loved ones, and, in the most extreme cases, risking one's life in combat. This level of commitment is reinforced through rigorous training, the fostering of a strong sense of camaraderie, and the internalization of values such as honour, courage, and loyalty.

The idea of sacrifice in military duty extends beyond physical danger. It also encompasses the emotional and psychological toll that military service can take on individuals. Soldiers must often cope with the stress of combat, the loss of comrades, and the moral dilemmas that can arise in warfare. The duty to remain resilient and to continue performing one's responsibilities despite these challenges is a key aspect of military duty.

Duty to Country and Comrades

Military duty is deeply intertwined with the concepts of patriotism and loyalty to one's country. Soldiers are trained to view their service as a contribution to the defence of their nation's values, freedoms, and way of life. This sense of duty to the country provides a powerful motivation for military personnel, giving them a sense of purpose and direction.

In addition to duty to the country, there is also a strong emphasis on duty to one's comrades. The bonds formed between soldiers are often described as akin to familial relationships, with a deep sense of trust and mutual reliance. This camaraderie is a crucial element of military duty, as soldiers must be able to depend on one another for support and protection in life-threatening situations. The duty to protect and support one's comrades is a central tenet of the military ethos, fostering a sense of unity and collective responsibility.

Ethical and Moral Considerations

Military duty is not only about obedience and sacrifice but also about ethical and moral considerations. Soldiers are expected to conduct themselves with honour and integrity, both on and off the battlefield. This includes adhering to the laws of war, protecting non-combatants, and treating prisoners of war humanely. The duty to uphold these ethical standards is reinforced through military codes of conduct, training programs, and the enforcement of rules of engagement.

The ethical dimension of military duty can be complex, as soldiers may be confronted with situations where the right course of action is not clear-cut. For example, decisions made in the heat of battle can involve moral dilemmas, such as distinguishing between combatants and non-combatants or deciding whether to take potentially harmful actions to achieve a strategic objective. In such cases, the duty to act ethically must be balanced with the demands of the mission and the need to protect one's unit.

The Role of Duty in Building Character

Military duty is often seen as a means of building character and instilling values such as discipline, honour, and resilience. Through their service, military personnel learn the importance of selflessness, teamwork, and perseverance. The sense of duty instilled in soldiers serves as a guiding principle that shapes their actions and decisions, both during and after their military service. This commitment to duty can have a lasting impact, influencing how individuals approach challenges and responsibilities in other areas of their lives.

Duty in Civil Services

The Nature of Duty in Civil Services

Civil services play a vital role in the functioning of government and the delivery of public services. The concept of duty in civil services is centred on the principles of public service, accountability, and integrity. Civil servants are tasked with implementing government policies, providing essential services to the public, and upholding the rule of law. Their duty involves serving the public interest and ensuring that the administration operates efficiently, fairly, and transparently.

Public Service and the Common Good

At the heart of civil service duty is the commitment to public service and the common good. Civil servants have a duty to act in the best interests of the public, providing services that promote the welfare and well-being of society. This includes a wide range of responsibilities, from maintaining public infrastructure and administering social programs to ensuring public safety and upholding justice.

The duty to serve the public requires civil servants to act impartially and without bias. They must carry out their responsibilities with a focus on fairness, equality, and the equitable distribution of resources. This commitment to the common good is fundamental to the role of civil servants, as they are entrusted with the task of implementing policies that affect the lives of citizens and the overall functioning of society.

Accountability and Transparency

Civil servants are accountable to the public and to the democratic institutions they serve. This accountability is a key aspect of their duty, as it ensures that they carry out their responsibilities in accordance with the law and ethical standards. Civil servants must be transparent in their actions, providing information and explanations about their decisions and the use of public resources. This transparency helps build public trust in government institutions and promotes confidence in the administration.

The duty of accountability also involves being open to scrutiny and oversight. Civil servants are expected to respond to inquiries from elected representatives, the media, and the public, providing accurate and timely information about their work. They must also be willing to accept responsibility for their actions and decisions, including acknowledging and rectifying mistakes when they occur.

Integrity and Ethical Conduct

Integrity is a cornerstone of duty in civil services. Civil servants are expected to conduct themselves with honesty, integrity, and ethical behaviour in all aspects of their work. This includes avoiding conflicts of interest, refraining from using their position for personal gain and upholding the principles of justice and fairness. The duty to act with integrity is essential for maintaining the credibility and legitimacy of government institutions.

Ethical conduct in civil services also involves treating all individuals with respect and dignity, regardless of their background or status. Civil servants have a duty to provide services without discrimination and to ensure that the rights of all citizens are protected. This commitment to ethical conduct helps ensure that the administration operates in a manner that is just, inclusive, and respectful of the diversity of society.

The Role of Civil Servants as Policy Implementers

Civil servants play a crucial role in the implementation of government policies. Their duty involves translating the policies formulated by elected officials into practical actions and programs that benefit the public. This requires a deep understanding of the policy objectives, as well as the ability to navigate complex bureaucratic processes and coordinate with various stakeholders.

The duty to implement policies effectively and efficiently is a central aspect of the role of civil servants. They must ensure that public resources are used wisely and that programs are delivered in a manner that achieves the intended outcomes. This requires a combination of technical expertise, managerial skills, and a commitment to public service.

Balancing Political Neutrality and Public Accountability

Civil servants have a duty to remain politically neutral while carrying out their responsibilities. This neutrality is crucial for ensuring that public services are delivered impartially and that government institutions operate independently of political influence. Civil servants must serve the government of the day, regardless of their personal political beliefs, and implement policies in a fair and unbiased manner.

However, the duty of political neutrality must be balanced with the duty of public accountability. Civil servants are accountable to the public and must ensure that their actions are aligned with the principles of democratic governance. This involves being transparent about the decision-making process, providing accurate information to the public, and ensuring that government policies are implemented in a manner that is consistent with the rule of law and ethical standards.

The Role of Duty in Promoting Public Trust

Duty in civil services is essential for promoting public trust in government institutions. Civil servants are the face of the government, and their actions and conduct have a direct impact on how the public perceives the administration. By fulfilling their duties with integrity, accountability, and a commitment to the common good, civil servants help build confidence in the government's ability to serve the needs of its citizens.

Public trust is built on the expectation that civil servants will act in the best interests of the public and that they will carry out their responsibilities with competence and integrity. When civil servants fulfil their duties in a manner that is transparent, ethical, and responsive to the needs of the community, they reinforce the legitimacy of government institutions and strengthen the social contract between the state and its citizens.

Duty in both military and civil service contexts is characterized by a commitment to serving a cause greater than oneself. In the military, duty involves a profound sense of sacrifice, loyalty, and obedience, with a focus on protecting the nation and supporting one's comrades. It requires a balance between following orders and upholding ethical principles, often in life-threatening situations.

In civil services, duty is centered on public service, accountability, and integrity. Civil servants have a responsibility to implement government policies, provide essential services, and act in the best interests of the public. Their duty involves maintaining transparency, ethical conduct, and political neutrality, all while being accountable to the citizens they serve.

Both contexts highlight the importance of duty as a guiding principle that shapes individual actions and decisions. Whether in the military or civil services, the fulfilment of duty contributes to the functioning of institutions, the protection of society, and the promotion of the common good.

Duty, at its core, refers to a moral or legal obligation. Philosophically, it is deeply rooted in ethical frameworks such as deontology, which posits that actions are right or wrong based on adherence to rules, with individuals having duties to fulfil regardless of outcomes. Leaders and citizens alike have duties: leaders must protect, govern justly, and serve the welfare of the populace, while citizens are expected to obey laws, pay taxes, and contribute to the common good.

Immanuel Kant, one of the most influential philosophers on duty, argued that moral duty arises from an individual's commitment to universal moral laws – an idea known as the 'categorical imperative'. This notion is crucial to understanding governance, as leaders are bound by the duty to uphold the rights and well-being of the people they govern.

The Nature of Despotism

Despotism is a form of government or leadership where a single entity – either an individual or a ruling group – exercises absolute power, often in a cruel or oppressive manner. Unlike duty, which is founded on responsibility and ethical action, despotism represents the excessive and illegitimate use of authority. Despotic leaders often disregard laws, manipulate governance for personal gain, and suppress opposition through force, censorship, or coercion.

Historically, despotism has been synonymous with tyrannical rule, where the ruler operates without regard for justice or the welfare of the governed. Aristotle distinguished between kingship, which aligns with the welfare of the people, and tyranny (despotism), which serves only the ruler's interests.

Historical Transformations: From Duty to Despotism

Throughout history, many rulers have started with a strong sense of duty, only to descend into despotism as power and ambition overshadowed their responsibilities. This progression is often gradual, beginning with minor transgressions and evolving into systemic abuse of authority. Several historical examples illustrate this phenomenon.

Julius Caesar: From Republic to Empire

Julius Caesar is a prominent figure who exemplifies the transformation from duty to despotism. Initially a general of the Roman Republic, Caesar was celebrated for his military conquests and political reforms that aimed to strengthen Rome. However, as he gained power, his sense of duty to the Republic gave way to personal ambition. His crossing of the Rubicon in 49 BCE marked the beginning of the end of the Roman Republic. Declaring himself dictator for life, Caesar shifted from a leader serving Rome to one seeking to dominate it.

Though he implemented reforms that benefited the populace, such as revising the calendar and alleviating debt, his consolidation of power ultimately eroded the foundations of the Republic. His assassination in 44 BCE was, in part, an attempt to restore Rome to balanced governance.

The French Revolution and Napoleon Bonaparte

The French Revolution began with a sense of duty to establish liberty, equality, and fraternity, transitioning from despotic monarchical rule to a democratic system. However, the emergence of Napoleon Bonaparte showed how even proponents of liberty could descend into despotism. Napoleon, once hailed as a defender of the Revolution, eventually crowned himself Emperor of France in 1804. His reign, marked by military conquest and the suppression of political opposition, reflected the shift from duty-bound leadership to autocratic despotism.

Modern Despots: The Case of Robert Mugabe

More recently, Robert Mugabe's story offers a stark example of duty's descent into despotism. Initially celebrated as a hero of Zimbabwean independence, Mugabe was committed to improving the welfare of the country's black majority. However, over his decades-long rule, Mugabe's leadership became synonymous with corruption, economic mismanagement, and repression of opposition. Mugabe's failure to relinquish power and his consolidation of authority within an elite ruling class led to widespread poverty, human rights abuses, and international condemnation. What began as a sense of duty to free and govern his people became a despotic reign defined by violence and authoritarian control.

Psychological and Sociopolitical factors leading to Despotism

Several factors contribute to the transformation from duty-bound leadership to despotism. These factors often arise from personal, psychological, and sociopolitical conditions that make despotism more likely, even in systems emphasizing duty.

The Corrupting Nature of Power

The phrase 'absolute power corrupts absolutely', coined by Lord Acton, aptly describes a key psychological driver behind despotism. Leaders who begin with noble intentions often become intoxicated by the authority they wield, and a lack of checks on their power fosters an environment where despotism flourishes. Studies suggest that power has profound effects on behaviour, often leading to reduced empathy, heightened self-importance, and an increased desire to maintain authority. This explains why leaders who once displayed a strong sense of duty can gradually become despots as they consolidate power.

Weak Institutional Frameworks

Weak institutions also contribute to the rise of despotism. In strong democracies, systems like the judiciary, legislative bodies, and free press curb executive authority. However, in many systems, especially nascent democracies or autocracies, these institutions are either weak or complicit in upholding despotic rule.

The fall of the Roman Republic can be partly attributed to the weakening of the Senate and other political institutions meant to regulate leaders like Caesar. Similarly, Mugabe's prolonged rule in Zimbabwe was facilitated by the lack of independent institutions capable of holding him accountable.

Popular Support and the Cult of Personality

Despots often maintain power through the creation of a 'cult of personality', where their leadership is seen as indispensable.

This manipulation of the populace leads people to equate the leader's rule with national stability or prosperity. Leaders like Napoleon and Mugabe leveraged this dynamic to solidify their power, portraying themselves as irreplaceable figures.

When despotic leaders enjoy popular support – whether through manipulation, propaganda, or genuine loyalty – it becomes difficult to remove them from power. In such cases, the distinction between duty and despotism blurs as leaders convince both themselves and their followers that their rule, however authoritarian, is for the greater good.

Contemporary Despotism: Governance in the Modern Era

In the 21st century, despotism may not manifest as overtly as it did in previous centuries. Modern despots often employ more sophisticated mechanisms to consolidate power, such as manipulating democratic processes, co-opting economic systems, and using digital surveillance.

Digital Despotism

In the digital age, despotism has taken on new forms. Governments have unprecedented access to citizens' personal information through technology and surveillance. Countries like China have implemented extensive surveillance programs, using data to control and suppress dissent. The Chinese Social Credit System exemplifies how modern despotism uses digital tools to enforce compliance. While promoted as a way to maintain order, it exemplifies a form of digital despotism where the government exercises intrusive control over citizens' lives.

Erosion of Democratic Norms

Another form of contemporary despotism arises from eroding democratic norms within ostensibly democratic countries. Leaders may manipulate electoral processes, undermine judicial independence, or suppress freedom of the press to maintain power, even while paying lip service to democracy.

For instance, leaders in Hungary and Turkey have been criticized for weakening independent institutions and concentrating power in the executive branch, moving their countries closer to despotism while maintaining a façade of democratic legitimacy.

Mitigating Despotism: Upholding Duty in Governance

Given the propensity for power to corrupt, it is crucial to identify strategies to uphold duty in governance and prevent the rise of despotism.

Strengthening Institutions

The most effective way to mitigate despotism is by ensuring that checks and balances are robust. Independent judiciary systems, free press, and transparent electoral processes are essential to holding leaders accountable and preventing the consolidation of power.

Promoting Civic Engagement

Citizens must play an active role in holding their leaders accountable. Civic engagement – through voting, protesting, or participating in political discourse – is vital to preventing the rise of despotic rule. An informed and engaged populace makes it harder for a leader to subvert democratic processes for personal gain.

Encouraging Ethical Leadership

Leadership training that emphasizes ethical governance and prioritizes duty over personal ambition is also key. Encouraging leaders to act with integrity and providing them with tools to resist the temptations of power is critical in preventing the rise of despotism.

The relationship between duty and despotism is complex and often fraught with tension. History has shown that leaders can transform from duty-bound servants of the people into despotic rulers who prioritize their power above all else. Factors such as the corrupting nature of power, weak institutions, and manipulation of public opinion contribute to this shift.

In the modern world, despotism may take new forms, but the underlying dynamics remain unchanged. By strengthening institutions, promoting civic engagement, and encouraging ethical leadership, societies can prevent duty from descending into despotism, ensuring governance remains a force for the common good rather than a tool for oppression.

Duty, Despotism, and Morality in the Indian Context: Ethical Dimensions of Power and Responsibility

India's history, governance, and moral philosophy offer a rich framework for examining the interplay between duty, despotism, and morality. As the world's largest democracy, India is rooted in a tradition that emphasizes duty and ethical governance. Dharma, derived from ancient Indian scriptures, signifies the moral and righteous path that individuals and leaders must follow. However, India's history also reveals moments when rulers and leaders strayed from their duties, giving rise to despotism and undermining moral principles.

From ancient reigns of kings and empires to modern-day politics, the tension between duty and despotism in India has been influenced by both ethical governance and moral failures. This book explores the concepts of duty, despotism, and morality within the Indian context, examining how morality has shaped governance across different eras. By analyzing key historical figures, events, and contemporary issues, we assess how India's ethical frameworks have both upheld and challenged the balance between duty and despotism.

Defining Duty, Despotism, and Morality in the Indian Context

Duty in Indian Philosophy: Duty and Ethical Governance

In India, the concept of duty is deeply tied to dharma, which transcends mere obligation and encompasses moral righteousness, justice, and ethical conduct. Leaders are expected to uphold dharma, ensuring justice and welfare for all members of society, while citizens have a duty to contribute to the collective good.

Despotism in Indian History: When Power Corrupts

Despite the strong emphasis on Duty, Indian history has witnessed instances of despotism, where leaders deviated from their moral duties. Despotism in the Indian context often emerges when Duty is ignored, and rulers prioritize personal or political gains over the well-being of their subjects. Throughout

India's history, from ancient empires to colonial domination, despotism has reared its head in various forms. Whether through authoritarian rule, exploitation, or corruption, despotic leaders have undermined India's ethical traditions, leading to societal suffering and injustice.

Morality in Indian Governance: A Legacy of Ethical Responsibility

Morality in Indian governance is shaped by centuries of philosophical thought, from Vedic teachings to Gandhian principles of non-violence (*ahimsa*) and truth (*Satya*). These moral frameworks have been instrumental in shaping the idea of ethical leadership in India, providing both a foundation for just governance and a counter to despotic tendencies.

Mahatma Gandhi's emphasis on moral leadership during the Indian independence movement is one of the most significant examples of how morality can guide political action. His doctrine of *satyagraha* – the insistence on truth and non-violent resistance – challenged British despotism and inspired generations of Indian leaders to pursue justice through ethical means.

Chapter 2
Duty in Historical Context

Duty, as a moral and philosophical concept, transcends cultural boundaries, playing a central role in both Eastern and Western thought. While 'duty' often evokes notions of obligation or responsibility, its deeper implications extend to the ethical structures of societies, the legitimacy of authority, and the morality of individual action. From the earliest civilizations, both Eastern and Western cultures have contemplated duty, albeit through distinct lenses that reflect their unique values and worldviews. In this chapter, we explore the concept of duty in historical contexts, focusing on ancient Indian philosophy with its emphasis on Duty and juxtaposing it with Western philosophical traditions, particularly those of ancient Greece and Enlightenment thinkers. Through a comparative analysis, we illuminate the parallels and divergences in these philosophies and their broader implications for governance, ethics, and the human experience.

Ancient Indian Philosophy on Duty

In ancient Indian philosophy, duty is encapsulated in the concept of dharma. Unlike the narrow interpretation of duty as a mere obligation, duty extends beyond individual responsibility to embody the universal law that governs the cosmos, society, and personal behaviour. Derived from the Sanskrit root 'dhr', meaning 'to hold' or 'to sustain', dharma represents the moral and cosmic order that upholds the balance of life. It is the principle by which both rulers and citizens must abide – a force that dictates ethical conduct, social harmony, and even the inner spiritual development of the individual.

Historical manifestations of Duty and Despotism in India

The interplay between duty, despotism, and morality has shaped India's governance throughout its history. From ancient Indian empires to British colonial rule and post-independence India, the tension between moral duty and despotic rule has had lasting impacts on the nation.

Ashoka the Great: A moral transformation from Despotism to Duty

One of the earliest examples of the interplay between duty and despotism in Indian history is the reign of Emperor Ashoka (304-232 BCE). Initially known as a ruthless conqueror, Ashoka's early reign was marked by violence and despotism, particularly during the Kalinga War, where his forces caused massive destruction and suffering. However, after witnessing the devastation of the war, Ashoka experienced a moral transformation, adopting Buddhism and dedicating himself to duty. His shift from despotism to a duty-bound ruler is one of the most remarkable examples of moral governance in Indian history. Ashoka's reign thereafter was characterized by non-violence, social welfare programs, and religious tolerance. His legacy as a moral ruler is reflected in enduring symbols like the Ashoka Chakra and the Lion Capital, which continue to represent justice and ethical leadership in India today.

The Multifaceted Nature of Duty

The notion of duty is complex and multifaceted, woven into the very fabric of Indian thought. It is not a static or rigid rule but a dynamic principle that shifts according to one's age, caste, gender, and specific circumstances.

In many places, duty is intertwined with selflessness and detachment, emphasizing that adherence to dharma is paramount to maintaining both personal integrity and the cosmic order.

The King's Duty and Governance

In the context of governance, *Raja Dharma* (the duty of kings) is a critical component of ancient Indian political thought. The ruler, or king, was expected to uphold Duty as the highest law, ruling justly and ensuring the well-being of his subjects. The ancient Indian text, the *Arthashastra* by Kautilya (Chanakya), emphasizes the king's duty to maintain order, justice, and prosperity. While the text is pragmatic in its advice on governance, often leaning towards Realpolitik, it nonetheless recognizes the ruler's moral duty to safeguard his people and protect the ethical fabric of society.

Ashoka's adherence to dharma became a model for future rulers, illustrating how duty, when aligned with morality, can lead to enlightened and benevolent governance.

Duty in Western Philosophies

In contrast to the Indian conceptualization of Duty, Western thought on duty evolved along a different philosophical and historical trajectory. In the Western context, duty is often framed through deontological ethics, where actions are judged based on their adherence to moral rules or duties rather than their consequences. While early Western philosophers such as Socrates, Plato, and Aristotle grappled with questions of duty and justice, the Enlightenment period saw the crystallization of duty as a central tenet of moral philosophy, particularly in the works of Immanuel Kant.

Duty in Ancient Greek Thought: In ancient Greece, the idea of duty was intricately tied to the concepts of *areté* (virtue) and *eudaimonia* (flourishing or well-being). For Plato and Aristotle, living a good life was synonymous with fulfilling one's duty, both to oneself and to the *polis* (city-state). In Plato's dialogues, particularly the *Republic*, the philosopher envisions an ideal society where individuals perform their duties according to their abilities and roles. Each citizen, by adhering to their respective duties – whether as a ruler, guardian, or craftsman – contributes to the overall justice and harmony of the state.

Aristotle, in his *Nicomachean Ethics*, also discusses duty in relation to virtue and the concept of the golden mean, where moral excellence lies in moderation between extremes. For Aristotle, duty is not an externally imposed obligation but rather the result of cultivating virtues such as courage, temperance, and wisdom. Duty, therefore, is the natural expression of a well-ordered soul, where reason governs desires and the individual acts in accordance with both personal virtue and societal expectations.

The Greek emphasis on civic duty is perhaps best exemplified in the life and teachings of Socrates. Socrates viewed his role in Athenian society as one of moral duty – to question, provoke, and guide his fellow citizens towards greater ethical understanding.

His trial and subsequent execution, as depicted in Plato's *Apology*, highlight the tension between individual duty and state authority. Socrates' unwavering commitment to his moral duty, even in the face of death, underscores the importance of ethical responsibility as a guiding principle in Western thought..

Duty and Consequences: Selfless Action versus Moral Absolutism

Another key difference lies in the relationship between duty and consequences. In Indian philosophy, particularly as articulated in the *Bhagavad Gita*, duty is performed without attachment to the results. This notion of *nishkama karma* (selfless action) teaches that one must act according to one's Duty but not be swayed by the fruits of those actions. This emphasis on selflessness aligns duty with spiritual growth, where the individual transcends personal desires and ego.

In Kantian ethics, on the other hand, consequences are irrelevant to the moral value of an action. What matters is whether the action adheres to the moral law. Kant's moral absolutism insists that duty must be followed regardless of the outcomes, even if those outcomes may seem undesirable in specific situations. This approach contrasts with the more pragmatic and flexible understanding of duty in Indian philosophy, where the consequences of one's actions are often considered in the context of Duty.

Role of the Individual in Society: Communal versus Autonomous Duty

The Indian concept of Duty is deeply embedded in the communal and hierarchical structures of society. One's duty is often defined by their role within the broader social order, such as caste, family, or occupation. This communal understanding of duty reflects the collectivist ethos of Indian society, where individuals are seen as integral parts of a larger whole, and their actions contribute to the maintenance of cosmic and social harmony.

In contrast, Western conceptions of duty, particularly in Kantian ethics, emphasize the autonomy of the individual. Kant's moral philosophy is based on the premise that individuals are rational agents capable of determining their duties through the exercise of reason. This emphasis on individual autonomy reflects the Enlightenment's broader focus on personal freedom, rights, and the capacity for moral self-determination.

Duty, whether in the form of dharma in Indian philosophy or moral obligation in Western thought, has been central to the ethical frameworks that guide human behaviour and governance. While both traditions emphasize the importance of duty, they approach it from different philosophical perspectives – Indian thought views duty as contextual and integral to the cosmic and social order, while Western thought, particularly Kantian ethics, emphasizes universal and absolute moral laws. These differences highlight the richness and diversity of human approaches to morality, ethics, and responsibility. As we continue to explore the notion of duty in contemporary governance and moral philosophy, these historical foundations remain essential to understanding the complexities of ethical leadership and the enduring struggle to balance personal, social, and cosmic duties.

Chapter 3
Totalitarianism and the Struggle for Control

Historical Overview of Totalitarianism

Totalitarianism is a political system in which the state seeks absolute control over every aspect of public and private life. The term gained prominence in the 20th century, with the rise of regimes that sought to reshape society according to ideological blueprints, employing propaganda, censorship, and terror as tools of control. Notable examples include Nazi Germany, Fascist Italy, and the Soviet Union under Stalin – regimes characterized by the ruthless suppression of dissent and the subjugation of the individual to the collective will of the state.

The origins of totalitarianism can be traced to the convergence of several factors, such as technological advancements that enabled mass surveillance and communication and the political and economic crises that made populations susceptible to authoritarian solutions. Totalitarian regimes often emerge in times of upheaval, offering the promise of stability and national rejuvenation in exchange for the surrender of personal freedoms.

Abuse of Power

The abuse of power has marked some of the darkest chapters in human history. It occurs when individuals or institutions wield power in an unjust, oppressive, or exploitative manner.

While abuse of power can be found in various political and social contexts, it is particularly prevalent in totalitarian states, where power is concentrated in the hands of a single party or leader, allowing for unchecked control over nearly every aspect of life. In such regimes, the abuse of power manifests in various forms and has profound psychological, social, and economic impacts on individuals and communities.

Forms and Manifestations of Power Abuse in Totalitarian States

Totalitarian regimes are characterized by the absolute concentration of power, where the state seeks to control all aspects of public and private life. This centralization of authority creates an environment ripe for abuse, often with little or no accountability. The abuse of power in totalitarian states manifests in multiple forms, with political repression and economic exploitation being among the most pervasive and damaging.

Political Repression

Political repression is a hallmark of totalitarian states. It involves the use of force, coercion, and intimidation to suppress dissent, control the population, and maintain the regime's power. This abuse aims to eliminate opposition, quell potential threats, and ensure the absolute dominance of the ruling party or leader.

Censorship and Propaganda

Censorship is one of the primary tools of political repression in totalitarian states. The regime exercises strict control over information, regulating what can be published, broadcasted, or disseminated. This censorship extends to all forms of media, including newspapers, television, radio, and the internet. By controlling the flow of information, the state manipulates public perception, prevents the spread of dissenting ideas, and promotes the official ideology.

Alongside censorship, propaganda plays a crucial role in political repression. Totalitarian regimes use propaganda to glorify the state and its leader, instil fear of internal and external enemies, and create a narrative that justifies the regime's actions. Propaganda serves to indoctrinate the population, fostering loyalty and obedience while demonizing opposition groups. This manipulation of information stifles critical thinking and makes it difficult for alternative viewpoints to gain traction.

Surveillance and Invasion of Privacy

Totalitarian states employ extensive surveillance to repress political dissent. Surveillance systems, including secret police, informants, and advanced technology, monitor the activities of citizens, organizations, and even government officials. This pervasive surveillance creates an environment of fear and uncertainty, where individuals are constantly aware that their actions and communications are being monitored.

The invasion of privacy extends beyond the public sphere into the private lives of individuals. The state may monitor personal correspondence, tap phone lines, and use informants to gather information about people's beliefs, associations, and behaviours. This erosion of privacy serves to deter dissent and control the population by making it clear that any deviation from the regime's expectations could lead to severe consequences.

Arbitrary Arrests and Detentions

Arbitrary arrests and detentions are another common tactic of political repression in totalitarian states. Individuals perceived as threats to the regime – including political activists, journalists, intellectuals, and ordinary citizens – can be arrested without due process and detained indefinitely. These arrests are often carried out without formal charges, and detainees are frequently subjected to harsh interrogation, torture, and inhumane treatment.

The lack of an independent judiciary means those arrested have little recourse to challenge their detention. Show trials, if they occur, are often staged to create a facade of legality, but they are typically rigged to ensure predetermined outcomes. Arbitrary arrests and detentions instil fear in the population, silence dissent, and reinforce the regime's authority.

Execution and Exile

In extreme cases, political repression leads to the execution or exile of perceived enemies. Public executions, often after show trials, serve as a powerful tool of intimidation, demonstrating the regime's willingness to use lethal force to maintain control. Exile, whether internal or external, is used to remove dissidents from the social and political landscape, effectively silencing their voices and eliminating sources of opposition.

Economic Exploitation

Economic exploitation is another form of power abuse prevalent in totalitarian states. The regime's control over the economy allows it to manipulate resources for its benefit, often at the expense of the population. This exploitation manifests in various ways, including the centralization of economic power, forced labour, and the manipulation of resources for political gain.

Centralization of Economic Power

Totalitarian regimes often centralize economic power by nationalizing industries, controlling markets, and implementing state-directed economic planning. This centralization allows the regime to allocate resources according to its priorities, which may include building a powerful military, advancing the interests of the ruling elite, or maintaining political control. In such systems, the state's interests take precedence over the needs and welfare of the general population.

This centralization leads to widespread corruption, inefficiency, and resource misallocation. The ruling elite uses their control over the economy to enrich themselves and their supporters, while the majority of the population suffers from poverty, lack of access to essential goods and services, and economic inequality.

Forced Labour and Economic Coercion

Forced labour is a common form of economic exploitation in totalitarian states. The regime may use forced labour to achieve economic goals, such as building infrastructure or extracting natural resources. This labour is often extracted from marginalized groups, political prisoners, or the general population under the guise of national service or economic necessity.

In some cases, individuals are coerced into working in harsh and dangerous conditions, with little or no compensation, under the constant threat of punishment or imprisonment. Forced labour provides the state with cheap labour, punishes those deemed disloyal, and reinforces the regime's control over the workforce.

Manipulation of Resources for Political Gain

Totalitarian regimes often manipulate economic resources for political gain, using them as tools to reward loyalty and punish dissent. The regime may allocate resources such as food, housing, and healthcare – based on political loyalty, ensuring that supporters are well-provided for while denying basic necessities to those seen as disloyal.

This manipulation of resources creates a system of patronage and dependency, compelling individuals and communities to show loyalty to the regime in exchange for access to essential goods and services. This economic exploitation serves to reinforce the regime's power, as it uses economic incentives and punishments to control the population and maintain dominance.

Psychological and Social Impact on Individuals and Communities

The abuse of power in totalitarian states has profound psychological and social impacts on individuals and communities. The constant threat of surveillance, repression, and economic exploitation creates an environment of fear, paranoia, and mistrust. These conditions have long-lasting effects on mental health and social cohesion, leading to the breakdown of social trust and the erosion of community bonds.

Fear and Paranoia

The regime's use of surveillance, censorship, and repression instils a pervasive sense of fear in the population. People are constantly aware that they are being watched, and this knowledge compels them to conform to the regime's expectations. This fear becomes internalized as individuals learn to censor themselves, avoid certain topics of discussion, and refrain from expressing dissenting opinions.

Paranoia and Social Fragmentation

The regime's use of informants and surveillance fosters a sense of paranoia within society. Individuals are aware that anyone could be an informer, including neighbours, colleagues, and even family members. This paranoia leads to social fragmentation, as people withdraw from social interactions and become increasingly isolated. The breakdown of social trust prevents the formation of social bonds and hinders collective efforts to resist or challenge the regime's power.

Breakdown of Social Trust

The abuse of power in totalitarian states results in the breakdown of social trust, which is essential for the functioning of a healthy society. Trust is the foundation of social cohesion, allowing individuals to cooperate, communicate, and build relationships. In totalitarian states, the regime's use of repression, surveillance, and manipulation undermines this trust, leading to social disintegration and alienation.

Mechanisms of Enforcing and Perpetuating Abuse

Totalitarian regimes use various mechanisms to enforce and perpetuate their abuse of power. These mechanisms are designed to maintain control, suppress dissent, and ensure the regime's dominance over society. Two of the most notorious tools of totalitarian control are the secret police and show trials.

Secret Police

The secret police are a key instrument of repression in totalitarian states. They operate as the regime's enforcers, tasked with monitoring, investigating, and eliminating potential threats. The secret police engage in extensive surveillance, using informants, wiretapping, and other methods to track the activities of individuals and groups. This surveillance creates a pervasive atmosphere of fear and uncertainty, compelling people to conform to the regime's expectations.

Show Trials

Show trials are staged events designed to demonstrate the consequences of dissent and justify the regime's repressive actions. These trials are highly choreographed, with the accused found guilty regardless of the evidence or lack thereof. Show trials serve to instil fear in the population, discredit the opposition, and reinforce the regime's authority.

The abuse of power in totalitarian states manifests in various forms, including political repression and economic exploitation. The regime's use of censorship, surveillance, arbitrary arrests, and forced labour serves to maintain control, suppress dissent, and exploit the population for its benefit. These actions create an environment of fear, paranoia, and mistrust, undermining the social fabric of society.

Mechanisms such as the secret police and show trials are central to enforcing and perpetuating this abuse. The secret police use surveillance and intimidation to silence opposition, while show trials serve as public spectacles that legitimize the regime's actions and instil fear in the population.

The consequences of abuse of power in totalitarian states are far-reaching, affecting not only individuals and communities directly targeted but also the broader society. The breakdown of social trust, erosion of moral and ethical values, and perpetuation of fear and compliance create a legacy of trauma and alienation that persists long after the regime has fallen.

Understanding the mechanisms and impacts of power abuse in totalitarian states are essential for recognizing the dangers of unchecked authority and the importance of safeguarding human rights, justice, and the rule of law. It serves as a reminder of the need to remain vigilant against the concentration of power and to promote systems of governance that protect individual freedoms and promote the common good.

Chapter 4
Morality in Modern Society

In the rapidly changing dynamics of modern society, morality remains the foundation of ethical behaviour, governance, and interpersonal relationships. While debates about morality date back to antiquity, the rapid pace of social, political, and technological changes today necessitates a renewed focus on its application and understanding. Morality in contemporary times is influenced by complex ethical frameworks, socio-political realities, and global perspectives, all of which shape the moral landscape of individuals, institutions, and nations. In this chapter, we explore the multifaceted nature of morality in modern society, examining ethical frameworks that guide moral behaviour, specific challenges in contemporary India, and global perspectives on moral dilemmas facing societies worldwide.

Ethical Frameworks

Ethical frameworks serve as guiding principles that help individuals and societies navigate moral choices. These frameworks provide a structure for assessing the morality of actions, decisions, and policies, offering insights into the values and norms that underlie ethical conduct.

Deontological Ethics

Deontological ethics, derived from the works of Immanuel Kant, emphasizes the importance of duty and adherence to moral rules.

This framework holds that actions are morally right or wrong based on their intrinsic nature rather than their consequences. According to deontologists, certain actions – such as telling the truth or respecting human rights – are inherently moral, regardless of the outcome. In modern society, deontological ethics often underpins legal systems, human rights frameworks, and institutional codes of conduct, providing a sense of moral duty that transcends personal or utilitarian concerns.

For example, human rights legislation around the world is grounded in deontological principles. The idea that every human being has inalienable rights, irrespective of their social, economic, or cultural status, reflects Kant's insistence on universal moral laws. This ethical framework is crucial in maintaining fairness, justice, and moral integrity in institutions and governance.

Utilitarian Ethics

In contrast to deontological ethics, utilitarianism, popularized by thinkers like Jeremy Bentham and John Stuart Mill, evaluates actions based on their outcomes. This results-oriented approach has profound implications in policymaking, business, and public welfare initiatives, where ethical decisions often involve weighing the benefits and harms to various stakeholders.

In contemporary society, utilitarian principles are frequently invoked in public policy decisions. For instance, governments might implement policies that restrict individual freedoms – such as during public health crises – to ensure the well-being of the larger population. The COVID-19 pandemic brought this ethical tension to the forefront as countries balanced individual rights with the collective responsibility to safeguard public health.

Virtue Ethics

Virtue ethics, rooted in the teachings of Aristotle, shifts the focus from rules and outcomes to the development of moral character. According to this framework, morality is not simply about adhering to external laws or achieving desirable outcomes but about cultivating virtues such as honesty, courage, and compassion. Virtue ethics posits that a morally good person will naturally make ethical decisions because they possess virtuous traits that guide their actions.

In modern society, virtue ethics plays a significant role in leadership and education, where character development is often emphasized over technical competence. Leaders who embody virtues such as integrity, humility, and empathy are seen as more morally sound and trustworthy. In education, schools and universities often focus on character-building programs that promote ethical values alongside academic achievement.

Care Ethics

Care ethics, developed by feminist philosophers such as Carol Gilligan, emphasizes the importance of interpersonal relationships and the ethical responsibility to care for others. This framework critiques the often impersonal and abstract nature of traditional ethical theories, arguing that moral decision-making should be rooted in empathy, compassion, and the nurturing of relationships.

In modern society, care ethics has gained prominence in fields such as healthcare, social work, and education, where the well-being of individuals and communities is paramount. The moral imperative to care for the vulnerable—whether in family settings, hospitals, or communities – is a central tenet of care ethics and reflects the growing recognition of emotional intelligence and relational ethics in contemporary moral discourse.

Morality in Contemporary India

India, known for its rich philosophical traditions and diverse cultural landscape, faces unique moral challenges in the modern era. As a rapidly developing nation with deep historical roots in ethical thinking, contemporary India is a blend of traditional values and modern aspirations. The moral fabric of India is shaped by its religious diversity, socio-economic inequalities, and the ethical dilemmas posed by globalization, modernization, and technological advancement.

Traditional Morality and Modern Dilemmas

The moral values of contemporary India are heavily influenced by its ancient philosophical heritage, particularly the concept of dharma (righteous duty). However, modern India faces a tension between adhering to traditional moral frameworks and navigating the ethical complexities of a globalized world. Issues such as gender equality, caste-based discrimination, environmental degradation, and corruption challenge traditional moral norms, requiring a re-evaluation of how morality is applied in a rapidly changing society.

For instance, the persistence of the caste system, despite legal measures to curb discrimination, remains a significant moral issue in India. While the Indian Constitution guarantees equality for all citizens, caste-based violence and social exclusion continue to challenge the country's moral and ethical commitment to justice and human dignity. The tension between traditional hierarchical structures and modern egalitarian values creates moral dilemmas that are central to contemporary Indian society.

Corruption and Moral Accountability

Corruption is one of the most pervasive moral challenges in modern India. The moral fabric of Indian governance and public life is frequently strained by widespread corruption, which undermines the country's democratic ideals and erodes public trust in institutions. Corruption not only stifles economic growth but also perpetuates inequality, as the most vulnerable segments of society are often deprived of basic rights and services due to corrupt practices.

In response to these challenges, India has witnessed numerous anti-corruption movements, such as the India Against Corruption movement led by Anna Hazare, which called for greater transparency, accountability, and moral integrity in public life. While these movements have brought attention to the need for ethical governance, corruption remains a significant moral issue, highlighting the gap between moral ideals and the reality of governance in modern India.

Gender Equality and Women's Rights

Another critical area of moral discourse in contemporary India is the question of gender equality and women's rights. Despite legal reforms aimed at promoting gender equality, such as the passage of laws against domestic violence and sexual harassment, deep-seated patriarchal values continue to shape the moral landscape of India. Issues such as female infanticide, gender-based violence, and unequal access to education and employment opportunities reflect the moral challenges faced by women in contemporary Indian society.

The #MeToo movement, which gained momentum in India in 2018, brought to light the widespread issue of sexual harassment and abuse faced by women in various sectors, including entertainment, media, and politics. The movement sparked a national conversation about gender-based violence and the need for moral accountability in addressing systemic sexism. However, it also highlighted the moral complexities of navigating a society where traditional gender roles and modern aspirations for equality often clash.

British Colonial Rule: Despotism and the Denial of Moral Duty

The British colonial period represents one of the most prolonged and oppressive eras of despotism in Indian history. The British East India Company, and later the British Crown, ruled India through exploitation, systemic racism, and the denial of basic human rights. Despite claims of a civilizing mission, British rule was marked by moral failures, as economic exploitation and political repression took precedence over the welfare of the Indian population. Famines, such as the Bengal Famine of 1943, were exacerbated by British policies, revealing the extent to which despotism overshadowed any sense of moral duty to the Indian people. Leaders like Mahatma Gandhi and Jawaharlal Nehru fought against this despotism, emphasizing morality, non-violence, and the ethical duty to achieve independence.

Indira Gandhi and the Emergency: A Case of Modern Despotism

In post-independence India, one of the most notable examples of the tension between duty and despotism occurred during the Emergency (1975-77), declared by Prime Minister Indira

Gandhi. Initially, Indira Gandhi rose to power with a strong sense of duty to uplift India, introducing several progressive policies. However, facing political challenges and accusations of electoral malpractice, she suspended democratic norms and assumed near-total control of the government. The Emergency marked a period of censorship, mass arrests, and curtailment of civil liberties, reflecting a temporary lapse into despotism. Gandhi's suspension of the Constitution and her authoritarian measures during this period led to widespread criticism and her eventual political downfall. This episode highlights the dangers of consolidating power and abandoning the ethical foundations of democracy, even with initially noble intentions.

Moral Failings and the Rise of Despotism in Modern Indian Politics

In modern India, even with robust democratic institutions, the interplay between duty and despotism remains relevant. Corruption, authoritarian tendencies, and the erosion of moral governance continue to pose challenges to India's political landscape.

Corruption and the Erosion of Moral Duty

Corruption remains a significant issue in Indian governance, undermining the moral duties of public officials. From bureaucratic inefficiency to large-scale political scandals, corruption erodes public trust in leadership and weakens the ethical foundations of governance. Corruption represents a modern form of despotism, where personal or political gain takes precedence over the welfare of the people, violating the principles of Duty and Morality.

The Manipulation of Nationalism and Populism

In contemporary Indian politics, populist leaders have at times used nationalism to manipulate moral values for political gain. While patriotism and national unity are important, the use of these sentiments to justify authoritarian measures or to suppress dissent can be seen as a form of moral despotism. The erosion of democratic norms, press freedom, and judicial independence in the name of national security or development raises ethical concerns about balancing duty to the nation with the preservation of individual rights and freedoms.

The Role of Morality in upholding Duty and preventing Despotism in India

Given the historical and modern challenges of despotism, the role of morality in governance remains crucial to ensuring that leaders uphold their duties ethically. India's rich philosophical traditions and democratic frameworks offer valuable tools for navigating these challenges.

Strengthening Democratic Institutions and Moral Accountability

One of the most effective ways to prevent despotism is by ensuring that India's democratic institutions remain strong and independent. The judiciary, Election Commission, and media must continue to act as moral guardians, holding leaders accountable for their duties and preventing the consolidation of despotic power. Upholding the rule of law and protecting the rights of citizens are essential to maintaining moral governance.

Reviving Gandhian Principles of Ethical Leadership

The legacy of Mahatma Gandhi's moral leadership remains a powerful guide for contemporary India. His emphasis on non-violence, truth, and ethical responsibility provides a framework for resisting authoritarianism and promoting social justice. Political leaders and citizens alike can look to Gandhian principles as a moral compass in times of political and ethical uncertainty.

Civic Engagement and Moral Responsibility

In a democracy as vast and diverse as India's, civic engagement plays a vital role in ensuring that leaders are held accountable for their duties. Citizens have a moral responsibility to participate in the democratic process, from voting to activism, ensuring that governance remains rooted in ethical principles. By actively engaging in the political process, Indian citizens can prevent the rise of despotism and promote a more just and moral society.

The concepts of duty, despotism, and morality are deeply intertwined in the Indian context, shaped by centuries of philosophical thought and political experience. From ancient rulers like Ashoka to modern leaders like Mahatma Gandhi, India's history is rich with examples of how morality has influenced governance, for better or worse.

While India's democratic institutions have helped mitigate despotism, challenges like corruption, authoritarian tendencies, and the manipulation of moral values continue to threaten ethical governance.

Environmental Ethics and Sustainability

India's rapid industrialization and urbanization have led to significant environmental challenges, raising important moral questions about sustainability and the ethical use of natural resources. The degradation of India's air, water, and land due to pollution, deforestation, and overexploitation of resources has brought environmental ethics to the forefront of public discourse. Issues such as air pollution in cities like Delhi, the destruction of forests for industrial projects, and the displacement of indigenous communities highlight the moral tension between economic development and environmental sustainability.

The moral imperative to protect the environment is rooted in India's spiritual traditions, which emphasize the interconnectedness of all life forms and the need for harmony between humans and nature. However, modern India's pursuit of economic growth has often led to environmental degradation, creating moral dilemmas about how to balance development with the ethical responsibility to preserve the environment for future generations.

Global Perspectives on Morality

In an increasingly interconnected world, moral challenges are no longer confined to national borders. Globalization, technological advancement, and transnational issues such as climate change, migration, and human rights violations necessitate a global perspective on morality. The ethical frameworks that guide individuals and societies must now address moral dilemmas that transcend local or national concerns, raising questions about universal moral values and the role of international institutions in promoting ethical behaviour.

Human Rights and Global Justice

The concept of human rights has become a cornerstone of global morality, providing a universal framework for assessing ethical behaviour across cultures and nations. The Universal Declaration of Human Rights, adopted by the United Nations in 1948, asserts the inalienable rights of all individuals, regardless of their nationality, race, or gender. This global commitment to human dignity reflects a shared moral vision of justice and equality that transcends cultural differences.

However, the application of human rights principles is often fraught with moral complexities. Issues such as the refugee crisis, human trafficking, and racial injustice challenge the ability of global institutions to uphold moral ideals in the face of political, economic, and social realities. The moral imperative to protect human rights is often at odds with national interests, leading to debates about the role of global governance in addressing ethical challenges on a transnational scale.

Global Inequality and Ethical Responsibility

Economic inequality is another major moral issue facing the global community. The widening gap between rich and poor, both within and between countries, raises ethical questions about the distribution of wealth and resources. Global poverty, access to healthcare, and educational disparities are not only economic issues but also moral concerns that demand attention from governments, international organizations, and civil society.

The moral responsibility of wealthy nations and individuals to address global inequality is a central theme in contemporary ethical debates. Initiatives such as international development aid, debt relief, and philanthropic efforts seek to address these disparities, but they also raise questions about the ethical implications of power dynamics in the global economy. The moral imperative to reduce inequality is complicated by the economic interests of powerful nations and corporations, leading to ongoing discussions about how to create a more just and equitable global system.

Climate Change and Environmental Ethics

Climate change is perhaps the most pressing moral issue of the 21st century, with far-reaching implications for future generations and the planet as a whole. The ethical responsibility to mitigate the effects of climate change has sparked global movements advocating for sustainability, conservation, and the transition to renewable energy sources. However, the moral burden of addressing climate change is unevenly distributed, with developing countries often bearing the brunt of its impact despite contributing less to global emissions.

The ethical debates surrounding climate change centre on questions of justice, responsibility, and intergenerational ethics. How should the global community allocate responsibility for reducing emissions? What moral obligations do wealthy nations have to support developing countries in adapting to climate change? And how should individuals, corporations, and governments balance economic growth with environmental sustainability? These are some of the critical moral questions that define the global discourse on climate change.

Morality in modern society is a complex and multifaceted concept shaped by diverse ethical frameworks, cultural traditions, and global challenges. In contemporary India, moral dilemmas surrounding corruption, gender equality, and environmental sustainability reflect the tension between traditional values and modern realities. On a global scale, issues such as human rights, inequality, and climate change demand a re-evaluation of moral responsibilities in an interconnected world.

As societies continue to evolve, the role of morality remains central to ensuring ethical behaviour in governance, social interactions, and global affairs. By drawing on both traditional and contemporary ethical frameworks, individuals and institutions can navigate the moral complexities of modern life, striving to create a more just, equitable, and sustainable world.

The Moral Justification of Totalitarian Regimes

Totalitarian regimes, despite their repressive and authoritarian nature, often provide moral justifications for their rule. These regimes use various ideological rationalizations to legitimize their authority, policies, and actions. By presenting themselves as the embodiment of a higher moral or ideological purpose, they seek to suppress dissent and win compliance or even support from the populace. However, these justifications are fraught with contradictions, as the actions of totalitarian states often starkly contrast with the moral and ethical principles they claim to uphold.

Ideological Rationalizations

Totalitarian regimes rely heavily on ideology to provide a framework for their rule and justify the concentration of power. These ideologies serve as a set of beliefs and values that guide the actions of the regime and define the goals of the state. By framing their rule within a specific ideological context, totalitarian regimes attempt to create a sense of moral legitimacy, presenting their actions as necessary and just.

Nationalism and Protection of the State

One of the most common ideological rationalizations used by totalitarian regimes is the concept of nationalism and the protection of the state. These regimes often portray themselves as the defenders of the nation, emphasizing the importance of national unity, security, and sovereignty. They claim that their repressive measures are necessary to protect the nation from internal and external threats, such as political dissidents, ethnic or religious minorities, or foreign enemies.

By framing their policies as a defence of the nation, totalitarian regimes seek to legitimize their use of force, censorship, and surveillance. This ideology often involves the creation of an 'us versus them' mentality, positioning the regime as the protector of the 'true' nation against perceived enemies. This can lead to the persecution of minority groups, political opponents, and anyone deemed a threat to the regime's conception of national identity.

Revolutionary Ideology and the Promise of Utopia

Many totalitarian regimes employ revolutionary ideology to justify their rule, particularly in communist and fascist states. The regime presents itself as the vanguard of a revolutionary movement aimed at creating a new social order. The promise of utopia serves as a powerful motivator, justifying the use of extreme measures in the pursuit of the revolutionary goal. The regime argues that the sacrifices and suffering of the present are necessary for the realization of a future society that will be just, prosperous, and harmonious.

The revolutionary ideology often involves a narrative of historical inevitability, where the regime claims to be the agent of an inevitable and righteous transformation of society. By positioning itself as the embodiment of the revolutionary ideal, the regime seeks to command loyalty and obedience from the population, even in the face of harsh and repressive measures.

The Cult of Personality

The cult of personality is another ideological tool used by totalitarian regimes to justify their rule. In many totalitarian states, the leader is elevated to a near-divine status, portrayed as a visionary, a saviour, or an infallible guide for the nation. This deification of the leader serves to legitimize the regime's actions, as the leader's decisions are presented as the manifestation of a higher wisdom or moral authority.

The cult of personality is reinforced through propaganda, state-controlled media, and education, creating a narrative that glorifies the leader and instils loyalty and reverence among the population. By associating the regime's actions with the leader's supposed infallibility, totalitarian states seek to justify their policies and suppress dissent.

The Moral Superiority of the Ideology

Totalitarian regimes often claim moral superiority for their ideology, arguing that their system of governance is based on higher ethical principles than those of other political systems. This claim of moral superiority is used to justify repressive measures, presented as necessary for upholding the greater good or moral order. By asserting the moral superiority of their ideology, totalitarian regimes seek to create a moral imperative for their actions and justify the suppression of dissenting views.

Contradictions within the Ideology

While totalitarian regimes attempt to provide moral justifications for their rule, these justifications are often riddled with contradictions. The actions of totalitarian states frequently conflict with the moral and ethical principles they claim to uphold, revealing the inherent hypocrisy and self-serving nature of their ideological rationalizations.

The Discrepancy Between Ideology and Reality

One of the most glaring contradictions is the discrepancy between the ideals these regimes espouse and the reality of their rule. Totalitarian states often promote lofty ideals such as equality, justice, and national greatness, yet their actions result in widespread oppression, inequality, and suffering. For example, communist regimes may claim to work toward a classless society, but in practice, they establish a new ruling elite that enjoys privileges and power at the expense of the broader population.

The Inconsistency of Moral Justifications

Totalitarian regimes employ moral justifications that are inconsistent and contradictory. They may invoke ethical principles such as justice, equality, or national security to legitimize their actions, but these principles are applied selectively and in ways that serve the regime's interests. For instance, a regime that claims to protect the rights of the people may systematically violate those rights through censorship, surveillance, and repression.

The Use of Fear and Coercion

Totalitarian regimes rely on fear and coercion to enforce their rule and ensure compliance with their ideology. This reliance on force contradicts the moral justifications the regime puts forward, as it reveals the regime's inability to command genuine loyalty or support from the population. The use of fear and coercion also leads to a culture of hypocrisy and deceit, where individuals are compelled to conform publicly to the regime's ideology while privately harbouring dissenting views.

The Moral Consequences of Totalitarian Rule

The contradictions within the ideology of totalitarian regimes have profound moral consequences for individuals and society. The regime's actions often result in widespread suffering, injustice, and the erosion of fundamental human values. The suppression of dissent, the violation of human rights, and the perpetuation of inequality undermine the moral principles the regime claims to uphold. The moral consequences extend beyond the immediate impact on individuals, contributing to the erosion of social trust and the breakdown of ethical norms.

Totalitarian regimes attempt to provide moral justifications for their rule through ideological rationalizations that frame their actions as necessary and just. These justifications often invoke concepts such as nationalism, revolutionary ideology, the cult of personality, and the moral superiority of the regime's ideology. However, these justifications are fraught with contradictions, as the actions of totalitarian states frequently conflict with the moral and ethical principles they claim to uphold.

The discrepancy between ideology and reality, the inconsistency of moral justifications, and the reliance on fear and coercion reveal the self-serving nature of totalitarian rule. These regimes use ideology as a facade to legitimize their concentration of power and suppress dissent, but their actions ultimately betray the moral bankruptcy of their justifications.

Understanding the contradictions within the ideology of totalitarian regimes is essential for recognizing the dangers of unchecked power and the importance of safeguarding principles of justice, human rights, and ethical governance. True moral legitimacy cannot be imposed by force or manipulation but must be rooted in the genuine pursuit of the common good and the protection of human dignity.

Morality in the Working Class Context

The working class struggle is not only an economic battle; it is also a moral one. Workers must navigate a complex moral landscape where the pursuit of survival and dignity often comes into conflict with systemic exploitation and injustice. This moral dimension is evident in the ways workers resist dehumanization and assert their right to be treated with respect and fairness.

The moral challenges faced by the working class are compounded by how power structures justify exploitation. Capitalist ideology, for instance, often frames economic success as a result of individual merit, implying that poverty is a consequence of personal failure. This narrative serves to obscure the systemic inequalities that disadvantage the working class and shifts the moral burden onto the individual rather than the system.

Abuse of Power and Working Class Exploitation

Abuse of power is a central theme in the working class struggle, as workers are often at the mercy of those who control the means of production. This power imbalance leads to various forms of exploitation, ranging from unsafe working conditions to inadequate compensation. Both corporations and governments have historically abused their power to suppress labour movements and maintain control over the workforce.

Examples of this abuse are numerous. In the early 20th century, industrialists employed private security forces to break strikes and intimidate workers while governments passed legislation to curtail union activities. In contemporary times, multinational corporations exploit labour in developing countries, using the threat of outsourcing to suppress wages and undermine workers' rights.

Cultural Representations of Working Class Struggle

The struggles of the working class have been powerfully depicted in literature, art, and film, serving both as a reflection of and a catalyst for social change. Works such as Upton Sinclair's *The Jungle* and John Steinbeck's *The Grapes of Wrath* have highlighted the harsh realities of working-class life, exposing the exploitation and injustices faced by workers.

These cultural representations play a crucial role in shaping public consciousness and fostering empathy for the working class. They challenge dominant narratives that valorize the wealthy and powerful, offering a counter-narrative that emphasizes solidarity, resistance, and the inherent dignity of labour. In doing so, they contribute to the ongoing struggle for justice and equality.

The relevance of the working-class struggle remains undiminished in today's globalized economy. While significant progress has been made in securing rights for workers, new challenges have emerged. The rise of the gig economy, for instance, has led to an increase in precarious employment, where workers lack job security and benefits. Similarly, globalization has resulted in the exploitation of labour in developing countries, where workers endure poor conditions and low wages.

In this context, the moral dimensions of the working class struggle are as pressing as ever. The fight for fair treatment, living wages, and safe working conditions continues as workers navigate an increasingly complex and uncertain economic landscape. Moreover, the abuse of power by corporations and governments remains a significant concern as efforts to undermine labour rights and suppress dissent persist.

PART 2

TOTALITARIANISM AND ABUSE OF POWER

Chapter 5
Historical Totalitarianism

Totalitarianism, characterized by its absolute control over every aspect of public and private life, represents one of the most severe forms of governance and abuse of power. This form of governance silences dissent, suppresses freedom, and controls the very thoughts and movements of citizens. While the most famous examples of totalitarianism occurred in 20th-century Europe with the rise of fascist regimes, elements of totalitarianism also existed in colonial contexts, notably in pre-independent India under British rule. Colonialism can be seen as a totalitarian structure imposed by foreign powers, using repression, exploitation, and manipulation to subjugate the colonized population. This chapter explores the rise and impact of totalitarianism, focusing on 20th-century fascist regimes, totalitarian aspects of British colonial rule in India, and the broader societal and cultural impacts of totalitarianism in both contexts.

Fascist Regimes of the 20th Century

The 20th century witnessed the rise of some of the most brutal and repressive totalitarian regimes in modern history, particularly under the banner of fascism. Fascism, a political ideology rooted in hyper-nationalism, authoritarianism, and

Chapter 5
Historical Totalitarianism

Totalitarianism, characterized by its absolute control over every aspect of public and private life, represents one of the most severe forms of governance and abuse of power. This form of governance silences dissent, suppresses freedom, and controls the very thoughts and behaviours of citizens. While the most famous examples of totalitarianism occurred in 20th-century Europe with the rise of fascist regimes, elements of totalitarianism also existed in colonial contexts, notably in pre-independent India under British rule. Colonialism can be seen as a totalitarian structure imposed by foreign powers, using repression, exploitation, and manipulation to subjugate the colonized population. This chapter explores the rise and impact of totalitarianism, focusing on 20th-century fascist regimes, totalitarian aspects of British colonial rule in India, and the broader societal and cultural impacts of totalitarianism in both contexts.

Fascist Regimes of the 20th Century

The 20th century witnessed the rise of some of the most brutal and repressive totalitarian regimes in human history, particularly under the banner of fascism. Fascism, a political ideology rooted in hyper-nationalism, authoritarianism, and militarism, emerged in the context of political and economic instability following World War I. This section will explore the rise and rule of fascist regimes, particularly those of Benito Mussolini in Italy and Adolf Hitler in Nazi Germany while considering their global significance.

Benito Mussolini and Fascism in Italy

Fascism first emerged as a political movement in Italy under Benito Mussolini, who capitalized on the social and political chaos of post-World War I Italy. With widespread economic instability and the perceived threat of communism, Mussolini's National Fascist Party gained support by promoting nationalism, militarism, and an authoritarian solution to Italy's woes. Mussolini's rise to power was marked by his infamous March on Rome in 1922, after which he became Prime Minister and eventually established a dictatorship.

Mussolini's totalitarian regime was characterized by the complete suppression of political opposition, the censorship of the media, and the use of propaganda to glorify the state and Il Duce (the Leader). Fascist Italy sought to control every aspect of public life, with an emphasis on creating a unified, militarized society. Mussolini's regime repressed civil liberties, using the secret police (Organization for Vigilance and Repression of Anti-Fascism or OVRA) to silence dissent. Cultural life was also tightly controlled, with art, cinema, and literature harnessed to promote fascist ideals.

One of the most significant aspects of Mussolini's totalitarian rule was his imperialist ambitions, which led to the invasion of Ethiopia in 1935. This expansionist drive reflected the fascist ideology of national strength through conquest, a theme that would later be echoed in Nazi Germany.

Adolf Hitler and Nazi Germany

Adolf Hitler's Nazi regime in Germany is often considered the most extreme example of totalitarianism in the 20th century. Hitler capitalized on the widespread dissatisfaction with the Weimar Republic and the economic devastation following World War I and the Treaty of Versailles. After becoming Chancellor in 1933, Hitler quickly dismantled democratic institutions and established a totalitarian dictatorship through the Enabling Act, which gave him sweeping powers.

Nazi totalitarianism was characterized by its absolute control over every facet of life. The regime promoted a hyper-nationalist and racist ideology that sought to establish the superiority of the 'Aryan' race. Hitler's government implemented anti-Semitic laws that stripped Jews of their rights, culminating in the genocide of six million Jews during the Holocaust.

The Nazi state controlled the media, education, and culture, using propaganda to indoctrinate the German population with Nazi ideology. Hitler's totalitarianism extended into the private sphere, where citizens were encouraged to inform neighbours and family members suspected of disloyalty. The Gestapo and SS created an atmosphere of fear and repression, ensuring that dissent was ruthlessly punished.

Nazi totalitarianism did not only devastate Germany but also plunged the world into World War II, leaving a legacy of destruction, human suffering, and genocide that shaped the post-war geopolitical order. The Holocaust, in particular, stands as one of the most horrific examples of state-sponsored terror and mass murder in human history.

Other Fascist and Totalitarian Regimes

While Mussolini and Hitler are the most prominent examples of fascist totalitarianism, other regimes in Europe and Asia exhibited similar totalitarian tendencies. Francisco Franco's Spain and Imperial Japan under Emperor Hirohito both demonstrated the use of authoritarian control, suppression of dissent, and militaristic expansionism, though not to the same ideological extremities as Nazi Germany.

In all these cases, totalitarianism reshaped not only political structures but also the cultural and social lives of those under their rule, demonstrating the devastating impact of the abuse of power.

Totalitarianism in Pre-Independent India

While India under British colonial rule did not experience totalitarianism in the form of fascist regimes, it was nonetheless subjected to a system of authoritarian and oppressive control that exhibited several characteristics of totalitarian governance. The British colonial regime sought to maintain strict control over Indian society, suppressing political dissent, manipulating the economy for imperial interests, and imposing cultural hegemony to justify and sustain its rule. Totalitarianism in pre-independent India manifested through repressive laws, censorship, economic exploitation, and cultural manipulation, all of which contributed to the subjugation of the Indian population.

British Colonialism as Authoritarian Rule

British colonial rule in India, particularly after the 1857 Rebellion, can be seen as a form of authoritarian control that shared certain features with totalitarian regimes. The British government established a bureaucratic system designed to extract wealth and maintain control over a vast and diverse population, often at the expense of Indian rights and freedoms.

The British imposed a range of laws that curtailed civil liberties, including the Rowlatt Act of 1919, which allowed for the detention of individuals without trial. This act sparked widespread protests, culminating in the Jallianwala Bagh Massacre, where British troops fired on unarmed protesters in Amritsar, killing hundreds. This act of brutality exemplified the repressive nature of British rule and its willingness to use extreme force to suppress dissent.

Moreover, British colonial administrators often ruled with an iron hand, limiting Indian participation in governance and suppressing nationalist movements through censorship, arrests, and exile. Prominent Indian leaders, including Mahatma Gandhi, Jawaharlal Nehru, and Subhas Chandra Bose, were frequently imprisoned for their political activities, while revolutionary groups faced harsh punishment under the colonial legal system.

Cultural Control and Manipulation

One of the key features of totalitarianism is the use of culture and education to promote state ideology and suppress alternative viewpoints. In pre-independent India, the British colonial administration sought to impose its cultural values on Indian society, often marginalizing Indian traditions and languages in favour of British norms.

The introduction of English as the medium of education and administration created a linguistic and cultural divide between the English-educated elite and the broader population. While British education policies introduced modern science and literature to India, they also served to create a class of Indians who were more aligned with British values, further entrenching British cultural hegemony. The famous statement by Thomas Babington Macaulay, who sought to create a class of persons, Indian in blood and colour but English in tastes, opinions, morals, and intellect, illustrates the manipulative nature of British educational policies.

Additionally, the British sought to control the narrative of Indian history and culture, presenting themselves as benevolent rulers bringing civilization to a 'backward' society. This distorted portrayal of Indian culture was used to justify British rule and suppress nationalist calls for self-determination.

Economic Exploitation and Social Control

Economic exploitation was another significant aspect of British colonial rule that mirrored totalitarian control. The British Empire systematically extracted wealth from India, often exacerbating poverty and famine in the process. The Bengal Famine of 1943, which resulted in the deaths of approximately three million people, was worsened by British policies that prioritized the export of food for the war effort over the needs of the Indian population. This economic exploitation, combined with the oppressive taxation system, deepened the poverty and inequality that persisted throughout the colonial period.

British rule also reinforced social divisions, particularly through its relationship with the Indian caste system. While the British did not create the caste system, they manipulated it to serve their administrative needs, co-opting upper-caste elites into the colonial bureaucracy and further entrenching social hierarchies. This divide-and-rule strategy served to fragment Indian society, making it easier for the British to maintain control.

Impact on Society and Culture

Totalitarianism, whether in the fascist regimes of Europe or the colonial context of India, left an indelible mark on society and culture. The suppression of dissent, the control of culture, and the manipulation of social structures had profound effects on the populations living under these regimes. This section examines how totalitarianism reshaped the social fabric, cultural identity, and intellectual life in both European and Indian contexts.

Suppression of Political and Cultural Dissent

Totalitarian regimes, by their very nature, seek to suppress any form of dissent, whether political or cultural. In Nazi Germany, the state tightly controlled artistic expression, banning 'degenerate' art that did not conform to Nazi ideology. Jewish artists, intellectuals, and writers were persecuted, their works destroyed, and their voices silenced.

In British-ruled India, political dissent was similarly suppressed. Indian newspapers and journals that criticized British rule were frequently censored, and leaders of the independence movement were regularly imprisoned. The British colonial government sought to maintain its control by limiting freedom of speech and assembly, ensuring that nationalist sentiments were kept in check.

However, in both contexts, the suppression of dissent often provoked resistance. In Nazi Germany, underground resistance movements emerged to challenge the regime, while in India, figures like Gandhi and Nehru mobilized the masses through civil disobedience, non-violent protest, and political activism.

These resistance movements sought to reclaim cultural and political autonomy from totalitarian control.

Cultural Revival and Nationalism in India

One of the most significant impacts of British totalitarian control in India was the eventual resurgence of Indian culture and nationalism. While the British sought to impose their cultural values, the independence movement sparked a cultural revival that sought to reclaim Indian identity. This revival was seen in the arts, literature, and education, where Indian intellectuals and artists began to celebrate Indian traditions, languages, and philosophies.

The cultural renaissance that followed the Independence movement was a direct response to the cultural suppression experienced under British rule. Figures like Rabindranath Tagore, who won the Nobel Prize in Literature in 1913, played a critical role in promoting Indian culture and challenging the cultural hegemony of the British. Tagore's works, along with those of other nationalist thinkers, sought to articulate an Indian identity that was distinct from the colonial narrative imposed by the British.

Similarly, the Swadeshi movement, which promoted Indian goods and boycotted British products, was not only an economic protest but also a cultural one. It emphasized self-reliance and the revival of traditional Indian crafts and industries, symbolizing a rejection of colonial economic and cultural control.

The Psychological and Social Impact of Totalitarianism

Totalitarianism not only reshapes political and cultural structures but also has a profound psychological impact on the populations it controls. In both Nazi Germany and colonial India, the constant surveillance, repression, and fear created an atmosphere of distrust and anxiety. People were often forced to conform to the state's demands at the cost of their personal freedoms and moral integrity.

In India, the psychological toll of colonial rule was compounded by the racial hierarchies imposed by the British. The systematic denigration of Indian culture and the promotion of British superiority led to a sense of alienation among many Indians, particularly among the educated classes who had been exposed to Western ideals but were denied political participation.

Despite these challenges, the resilience of the Indian people in the face of British totalitarianism ultimately contributed to the success of the Independence movement. The psychological impact of colonialism, while profound, also fostered a spirit of resistance and self-determination that would shape the course of modern Indian history.

The history of totalitarianism, whether in the form of 20th-century fascist regimes or the colonial control of India, highlights the devastating consequences of the abuse of power. Totalitarian regimes seek to control every aspect of life, from politics to culture, often leading to widespread repression, suffering, and loss of freedom. In both Europe and India, totalitarianism left a deep scar on society, reshaping cultural identities and social structures in ways that continue to resonate today.

In pre-independent India, the British colonial regime exhibited several characteristics of totalitarianism, using censorship, repression, and cultural manipulation to maintain its control. However, the Indian people's resilience in the face of this oppression ultimately led to the resurgence of Indian culture and the successful struggle for independence.

By understanding the historical contexts of totalitarianism, we can better appreciate the importance of safeguarding individual freedoms, cultural diversity, and democratic values in the face of modern authoritarianism. As we confront new challenges in the 21st century, the lessons of historical totalitarianism remind us of the enduring need to protect human rights, promote justice, and resist the concentration of power in the hands of the few.

Chapter 6
Contemporary Totalitarianism

Totalitarianism, traditionally defined as a centralized and dictatorial regime that seeks to control every aspect of public and private life, has evolved significantly in contemporary times. Modern totalitarian regimes, while employing different methods and approaches compared to their historical counterparts, continue to maintain their grip on power through propaganda, suppression of dissent, and the manipulation of democratic institutions. This chapter explores the nature of modern-day dictatorships, the infiltration of totalitarian tendencies in democracies, and specific case studies of abuse of power, focusing on India and the global context.

Modern-Day Totalitarianism

Totalitarianism has not disappeared but has evolved to fit the contours of the modern world. In the digital age, surveillance and control have taken on new forms, with technology being used to monitor, manipulate, and suppress individuals on an unprecedented scale. States and corporations alike collect vast amounts of data, using it to shape behaviour and restrict freedoms in ways that echo the practices of past totalitarian regimes.

One of the most concerning aspects of modern-day totalitarianism is the use of technology for mass surveillance. Governments employ sophisticated tools to monitor communications, track movements, and gather information on individuals, often in the name of national security. This erosion of privacy and personal freedom has significant implications for democracy and civil liberties, raising questions about the balance between security and individual rights.

Duty in Contemporary Society

The concept of duty has evolved in contemporary society, reflecting the complexities of a globalized world. While traditional notions of duty, such as loyalty to family and nation, remain relevant, there is an increasing emphasis on individual autonomy and personal responsibility. People are encouraged to pursue their own goals and contribute to society in ways that align with their values and interests.

However, this shift towards individualism has also created new tensions. In a world where personal freedom is highly valued, there is often a reluctance to accept duties that require self-sacrifice or limit personal choice. This has led to debates about the nature and extent of one's duty to others, particularly in areas such as social justice, environmental responsibility, and public health.

Working Class and Morality Today

The moral dimensions of the working-class struggle remain a central concern in contemporary society. The gig economy, characterized by short-term contracts and freelance work, has created a precarious labour market where workers lack job security and benefits. This raises questions about the ethical treatment of workers and the responsibilities of employers in ensuring fair and equitable working conditions.

Moreover, the globalization of labour has raised significant moral questions about the exploitation of workers in developing countries. Multinational corporations often seek to minimize costs by outsourcing production to countries with lower labour standards, resulting in poor working conditions and low wages. This has sparked a global movement for ethical consumption and corporate accountability, as consumers and activists call for fair treatment of workers and sustainable business practices.

Abuse of Power in the Modern Context

Abuse of power remains a pervasive issue in contemporary society, manifesting in various forms, from corporate misconduct to political corruption. In the corporate world, power is often concentrated in the hands of a few individuals or entities, leading to practices that prioritize profit over the well-being of workers, consumers, and the environment. This is evident in cases of labour exploitation, environmental degradation, and unethical business practices.

Political abuse of power also persists, as governments and leaders use their authority to suppress dissent, manipulate information, and maintain control. This is particularly evident in authoritarian regimes, where the state's power is used to silence opposition and maintain a monopoly on truth. However, even in democratic societies, concerns about abuse of power are growing as issues such as mass surveillance, political corruption, and the erosion of civil liberties come to the forefront.

The Ongoing Struggle for Justice and Equity

The struggle for justice and equity is an ongoing process as individuals and movements continue to challenge the abuse of power and advocate for the rights of the marginalized. In recent years, there has been a resurgence of activism around issues such as workers' rights, racial justice, gender equality, and environmental sustainability. These movements seek to address systemic inequalities and abuses of power, calling for a more just and equitable world. At the heart of this struggle is a moral imperative to uphold the dignity and rights of all individuals. It is a call to recognize our shared humanity and to take collective action to dismantle the structures of power that perpetuate inequality and injustice. In this sense, the themes of duty, totalitarianism, working-class struggle, morality, and abuse of power remain as relevant today as ever, serving as a reminder of the ongoing need for vigilance, resistance, and the pursuit of a more just society.

Modern-Day Dictatorships

The Evolution of Totalitarianism

Modern totalitarian regimes have adapted to the changing global landscape. Unlike the overtly oppressive regimes of the 20th century, contemporary dictatorships use more sophisticated means of maintaining control. While the classic hallmarks of totalitarianism – state control of the media, propaganda, and the suppression of opposition – persist, modern regimes also exploit technology and globalization to entrench their power.

Countries like Russia and China demonstrate that totalitarian control can coexist with economic modernization and integration into the global economy. This evolution challenges the notion that economic liberalization inevitably leads to political liberalization. Modern dictatorships often allow limited economic freedom and participation in international markets while maintaining strict control over political and social life.

State Control in the Digital Age

In the digital era, methods of surveillance and control have become more pervasive and sophisticated. Governments have harnessed technology to monitor their citizens, censor information, and suppress dissent. China's extensive surveillance network, including the use of facial recognition and the Social Credit System, exemplifies how technology can be used to enforce social conformity and loyalty to the state.

Similarly, Russia's use of cyber tactics to manipulate information and influence political outcomes—both domestically and abroad—highlights the new dimensions of control in modern totalitarian regimes. These regimes use a combination of cyber surveillance, data collection, and internet censorship to keep their populations in check. The 'Great Firewall of China' is a prime example of how a state can control and manipulate the flow of information, ensuring that only state-sanctioned narratives reach the public.

The Facade of Democracy

Many modern-day dictatorships maintain a facade of democracy, conducting elections and maintaining institutions like parliaments and courts. However, these democratic processes are often manipulated to ensure the ruling party's dominance. Elections may be held, but they are neither free nor fair. Opposition parties are harassed, dissenting voices are silenced, and media outlets are either state-controlled or heavily censored.

In countries like Turkey and Hungary, governments have used legal mechanisms and constitutional changes to consolidate power while maintaining a veneer of democratic legitimacy. These regimes often justify their actions by invoking national security, economic stability, or cultural preservation. The result is a form of governance that is authoritarian in nature but camouflaged by democratic institutions and rhetoric.

Modern-day dictatorships are characterized by authoritarian control, a lack of political freedoms, and centralized power, often maintained through repression. Here are some examples:

North Korea (Democratic People's Republic of Korea): Led by Kim Jong-un, North Korea is a highly centralized totalitarian state with strict control over all aspects of life, including political expression, media, and economic activities. The regime uses propaganda, fear, and military strength to maintain power.

Belarus: President Alexander Lukashenko has ruled Belarus since 1994. His government is known for controlling the media, rigging elections, and suppressing political dissent, especially during the 2020 presidential election, which was widely criticized as fraudulent.

Russia: Under Vladimir Putin, Russia has shifted toward an authoritarian regime, with power highly centralized in the presidency. Political opposition is suppressed, independent media are restricted, and dissent is met with arrests and persecution.

Syria: President Bashar al-Assad has maintained power since 2000, often through brutal measures, including military crackdowns on protests and opposition. The ongoing civil war and the regime's use of violence against civilians have underscored the dictatorial nature of Assad's rule.

Eritrea: President Isaias Afwerki has been in power since the country gained independence in 1993. Eritrea is often referred to as the 'North Korea of Africa' due to its lack of political freedom, indefinite military conscription, and repression of dissent.

China: While China officially has a one-party system led by the Communist Party, President Xi Jinping has consolidated power, effectively eliminating term limits and tightening control over all state institutions, the media, and civil society. Political dissent is not tolerated, and state surveillance is pervasive.

Turkmenistan: President Gurbanguly Berdimuhamedow (succeeded by his son Serdar Berdimuhamedow in 2022) has ruled Turkmenistan with near-total control, employing propaganda, censorship, and surveillance to suppress dissent and maintain his cult of personality.

We can include Iran in this list. Iran is an authoritarian state with a complex power structure that combines elements of theocracy with limited republican features. The country is officially an Islamic Republic, but power is highly centralized and controlled by unelected bodies, particularly under the authority of the Supreme Leader.

These countries illustrate different forms of modern-day dictatorships, where power is centralized, political freedoms are restricted, and the leadership often remains in control for extended periods, limiting any form of opposition or democratic processes.

Totalitarian Trends in Democracies

The Erosion of Democratic Norms

Totalitarian tendencies are not confined to overtly authoritarian regimes; they have begun to infiltrate democracies around the world. Populist leaders in several democratic countries have exploited economic anxieties, social divisions, and the spread of misinformation to undermine democratic norms and consolidate power. These leaders often attack the independence of the judiciary, restrict press freedom, and undermine the integrity of elections.

The use of propaganda and disinformation to manipulate public opinion is a key characteristic of this trend. In the digital age, social media platforms have become battlegrounds for controlling the narrative. Governments and political actors deploy bots, trolls, and fake news to create confusion, amplify divisions, and delegitimize opponents. This erosion of truth and fact-based discourse weakens the public's ability to hold leaders accountable and makes societies more susceptible to authoritarian influence.

Surveillance and Control in Democracies

In democratic states, the increasing use of surveillance and data collection by governments raises concerns about privacy and the potential for abuse. Under the pretext of counter-terrorism, crime prevention, or public health, many governments have expanded their monitoring capabilities, collecting vast amounts of data on their citizens. While these measures are often justified as necessary for national security, they also raise concerns about privacy and potential abuse.

The use of surveillance technology and data analytics can lead to a chilling effect on free expression, as individuals may self-censor out of fear of government scrutiny. The potential for abuse becomes even more significant when these tools are used to monitor political opponents, activists, and journalists. In this context, democracies must grapple with the delicate balance between security and the protection of civil liberties.

Let's discuss some examples of the Abuse of Power.

India: Democratic Backsliding and Centralization of Power

India, the world's largest democracy, has faced criticism for increasingly authoritarian tendencies under the leadership of the Bharatiya Janata Party (BJP) and Prime Minister Narendra Modi. Since coming to power in 2014, the BJP government has been accused of eroding democratic norms, centralizing power, and suppressing dissent.

Media and Press Freedom: The government has been accused of attempting to control the media through various means, including exerting pressure on journalists, encouraging self-censorship, and promoting pro-government narratives. Media outlets that criticize the government have faced legal challenges, raids by tax authorities, and withdrawal of government advertising, which is a major source of revenue for many media houses.

Use of Surveillance: India has expanded its surveillance capabilities with projects like the Central Monitoring System (CMS) and the Aadhaar biometric identification system. While these initiatives are presented as tools for national security and efficient governance, they raise concerns about privacy and the potential for misuse in monitoring and controlling dissent.

Curbing Dissent and Activism: The government has been criticized for its handling of protests and dissent, particularly the use of sedition laws, anti-terrorism laws, and the Unlawful Activities (Prevention) Act (UAPA) to detain activists, journalists, and students. The crackdown on protests against the Citizenship Amendment Act (CAA) and the farmers' protests are examples of how dissent is being increasingly criminalized in India.

Undermining Democratic Institutions: Concerns have been raised about the centralization of power and the undermining of democratic institutions such as the judiciary, the Election Commission, and independent agencies. The government's influence over these institutions has raised questions about their ability to function independently and impartially.

China: The Totalitarian Model

China, under the leadership of the Communist Party, has developed a sophisticated system of control that combines traditional totalitarian elements with modern technology. The regime's ability to maintain control over a vast and diverse population is a testament to its effective use of surveillance, propaganda, and legal mechanisms.

Surveillance State: China's extensive surveillance network, including the use of facial recognition, artificial intelligence, and big data analytics, is one of the most advanced in the world. The Social Credit System, which rates citizens based on their behaviour, is an example of how the Chinese Communist Party leverages technology to enforce conformity and loyalty. The regime's ability to monitor and control the population extends to controlling internet access and censoring online content.

Repression of Minorities: The treatment of Uighur Muslims in Xinjiang highlights the regime's use of totalitarian tactics to suppress minority groups. The Chinese government has established a network of re-education camps and employs facial recognition technology to monitor the population, aiming to eradicate cultural and religious practices deemed a threat to state ideology.

Media and Information Control: The Chinese government maintains strict control over the media, ensuring that only state-approved narratives reach the public. The 'Great Firewall of China' is a key tool in this effort, blocking access to foreign news sources and social media platforms.

Russia: The Return of Authoritarianism

Russia, under President Vladimir Putin, has become emblematic of the modern authoritarian state. Putin's regime has systematically dismantled democratic institutions and silenced opposition through a combination of legal manipulation, control over the media, and the use of force.

Manipulation of Elections: While Russia holds elections, they are widely regarded as neither free nor fair. The government controls the electoral process, ensuring that genuine opposition is marginalized or disqualified. The ruling party, United Russia, dominates the political landscape, and Putin's grip on power remains unchallenged.

Suppression of Dissent: The Russian government has a long history of suppressing political dissent and opposition.

This includes the assassination or imprisonment of political opponents and the use of anti-extremism laws to target activists and non-governmental organizations. The poisoning of opposition leader Alexei Navalny and the subsequent crackdown on protests highlight the regime's willingness to use violence and intimidation to maintain control.

Media Control and Propaganda: The Russian state exercises tight control over the media, using it as a tool to promote pro-government narratives and discredit opposition. Independent media outlets face constant pressure, including legal harassment, financial penalties, and physical attacks. The government also employs a sophisticated propaganda machine to influence public opinion and promote its geopolitical agenda.

Turkey and Hungary: The Drift Towards Illiberal Democracy

Turkey and Hungary represent cases where democratically elected leaders have eroded democratic norms and institutions to consolidate power, giving rise to what some analysts call 'illiberal democracy'.

Turkey under Erdoğan: Since the failed coup attempt in 2016, President Recep Tayyip Erdoğan's government has launched a widespread purge of perceived enemies, including military personnel, journalists, academics, and civil servants. Thousands were detained or dismissed from their jobs, and media outlets critical of the government were shut down. The government's control over the judiciary and its recent push to consolidate power through constitutional changes have further weakened

Turkey's democratic institutions and moved the country toward authoritarian rule.

Hungary under Orbán: Prime Minister Viktor Orbán's government has systematically undermined democratic checks and balances in Hungary. This includes curbing the independence of the judiciary, limiting press freedom, and altering the electoral system to favour the ruling party. Orbán's government has also used anti-immigrant rhetoric and nationalism to consolidate power, creating an environment where dissent is stifled, and opposition parties face significant obstacles in challenging the ruling regime.

United States: Democratic Erosion

Even established democracies like the United States have shown signs of democratic erosion. The 2016 and 2020 presidential elections exposed vulnerabilities in the country's democratic institutions, including the influence of foreign interference, the spread of disinformation, and attempts to undermine the integrity of the electoral process.

Polarization and Media Manipulation: The polarization of the media landscape, coupled with the rise of populist rhetoric and attacks on the legitimacy of the press and judiciary, has raised concerns about the resilience of democratic norms. The use of social media platforms to spread misinformation and the rise of echo chambers have contributed to a fragmented and polarized society, making it easier for authoritarian tendencies to take root.

Challenges to Electoral Integrity: The questioning of electoral outcomes and the spread of baseless claims about election fraud have undermined public trust in the democratic process. The events surrounding the 2020 presidential election, including attempts to overturn the results and the storming of the Capitol, have raised alarms about the stability of democratic institutions and the potential for further erosion of democratic norms.

Contemporary totalitarianism manifests in various forms across the globe, ranging from overtly authoritarian regimes to more subtle erosions of democratic norms in established democracies. In India, concerns about media freedom, the use of surveillance, and the centralization of power reflect a troubling trend of democratic backsliding. Globally, the use of modern technology, propaganda, and legal manipulation have allowed regimes to maintain control and suppress dissent with unprecedented efficiency.

These trends pose significant challenges to the principles of freedom, human rights, and democratic governance. As totalitarian tendencies continue to emerge and evolve, it is crucial for the global community to remain vigilant and proactive in defending democratic values and ensuring that the tools of modernity are used to enhance, rather than erode, the fundamental rights and freedoms of individuals.

Chapter 7
Control Mechanisms

The mechanisms of control in contemporary regimes have evolved significantly from the blunt instruments of earlier totalitarian states. Modern governments, whether authoritarian or democratic with authoritarian tendencies, utilize a range of sophisticated control mechanisms to maintain power. This chapter explores the nuances of surveillance and censorship, propaganda and media manipulation, and the psychological impact of these tactics on populations, focusing on India and drawing comparisons with global practices.

Surveillance and Censorship

Surveillance in the Digital Age In today's interconnected world, surveillance has become an essential tool for many governments, justified under the pretexts of national security, crime prevention, and public safety. The advent of digital technology has made it easier for states to monitor their citizens' activities, communications, and even thoughts. Surveillance now extends beyond the physical realm into the digital world, encompassing internet usage, social media, and even personal data stored on smartphones and other devices.

India's Surveillance Apparatus

India has developed an extensive surveillance apparatus over the years. The Central Monitoring System (CMS), implemented by the Indian government, is designed to allow law enforcement agencies to monitor all forms of digital communication, including phone calls, text messages, and emails. Although presented as a tool for combating terrorism and ensuring national security, the CMS has raised significant privacy concerns. Critics argue that it grants the government unfettered access to citizens' private communications without adequate oversight or judicial review.

In addition to CMS, the Aadhaar system, a nationwide biometric identification program, has been a contentious point of discussion regarding privacy and surveillance in India. While Aadhaar has been touted as a means to streamline government services and reduce fraud, it has also been criticized for creating a centralized database of biometric and personal information that could be used for surveillance purposes. The mandatory linking of Aadhaar to various services, including bank accounts and mobile numbers, has heightened fears of a surveillance state.

Global Comparisons Globally, countries like China and Russia have taken surveillance to extreme levels. China's surveillance state is one of the most sophisticated in the world, employing an extensive network of CCTV cameras, facial recognition technology, and AI algorithms to monitor its citizens. The Social Credit System further extends the state's reach by tracking individuals' behaviour, rewarding or punishing them based on their conformity to state-approved norms.

Russia, under President Vladimir Putin, has also developed a robust surveillance infrastructure. The System for Operative Investigative Activities (SORM) allows the Federal Security Service (FSB) to monitor all forms of digital communication. In recent years, the Russian government has passed laws requiring internet service providers to store users' data locally and provide it to the government upon request, significantly expanding state surveillance capabilities.

In comparison, Western democracies like the United States and the United Kingdom also engage in surveillance, albeit with more legal and judicial oversight. Programs such as PRISM and the use of the UK's Investigatory Powers Act (often referred to as the 'Snooper's Charter') have raised concerns about the balance between security and privacy. However, unlike authoritarian states, these countries have a relatively more transparent process and avenues for public and legal recourse.

Censorship: Controlling the Narrative

Censorship is a critical tool used by states to control the flow of information and shape public perception. By restricting access to information, governments can suppress dissent, eliminate opposition narratives, and maintain a monopoly on truth. The methods of censorship can vary from outright bans on certain types of content to more subtle forms of content moderation and self-censorship induced by the fear of retribution.

India's Approach to Censorship

India has a complex relationship with censorship, shaped by its democratic ethos and the challenges of managing a diverse and populous nation. The Indian government exercises control over information through legal mechanisms, including the Information Technology Act, the Cinematograph Act, and the Cable Television Networks Regulation Act. These laws give the government the authority to block websites, restrict the distribution of films and media content, and regulate broadcasting.

The government has also used these laws to justify internet shutdowns, a tactic that has been increasingly employed in recent years. India holds the dubious distinction of being one of the world leaders in internet shutdowns, with authorities frequently suspending internet services in regions experiencing unrest, such as Kashmir. These shutdowns are ostensibly carried out to maintain public order, but they also serve to suppress the flow of information and prevent the organization of protests.

Another aspect of censorship in India is the control over digital platforms. The government has pressured social media companies to comply with takedown requests and remove content deemed to be a threat to public order or national security. In 2021, the government introduced new IT rules that require social media companies to appoint grievance officers and provide traceability for certain messages, raising concerns about the potential for censorship and surveillance.

Global Comparisons

China is perhaps the most extreme example of state censorship, with the Great Firewall serving as a comprehensive system of internet regulation that blocks access to foreign websites, filters online content, and monitors internet usage. The Chinese government employs a vast network of censors who work tirelessly to remove any content that could be deemed subversive or contrary to state ideology. Social media platforms are heavily monitored, and any form of dissent or criticism of the government is swiftly suppressed.

In Russia, media censorship is more about control than outright bans. The government has established dominance over most mainstream media outlets, and independent journalism is heavily curtailed. The state uses a combination of legal pressure, intimidation, and propaganda to shape the media landscape. Online censorship is also on the rise, with laws that allow the government to block websites and restrict access to content deemed to be extremist or harmful to public order.

Even in democratic nations, there are instances of censorship, though they are typically framed within the context of national security or public morality. In the United States, for instance, the debate around censorship often revolves around issues like hate speech, misinformation, and the role of social media companies in moderating content. While there is a higher degree of freedom, concerns about the overreach of governmental and corporate power in censoring information persist.

Propaganda and Media Manipulation

The Role of Propaganda in Modern States

Propaganda is a powerful tool used by states to influence public opinion, shape political narratives, and legitimize their authority. It involves the dissemination of information – often biased, misleading, or false – designed to persuade or manipulate the populace. In the modern world, propaganda is not just about spreading positive messages about the state; it also involves discrediting opponents, creating fear or distrust, and fostering a sense of nationalism or unity.

India's use of Propaganda

In India, the use of propaganda has become increasingly sophisticated, especially with the rise of digital media. The government and political actors have employed various forms of propaganda to shape public perception, promote their agendas, and discredit opposition voices. This includes the use of social media, state-sponsored news outlets, and the strategic release of information.

Social Media and Troll Armies: Social media platforms like Facebook, Twitter, and WhatsApp have become battlegrounds for propaganda in India. The ruling party and its affiliates have been accused of using troll armies and fake accounts to spread misinformation, attack political opponents, and create a narrative that aligns with their ideological stance. The spread of fake news and disinformation on these platforms has been a significant issue, with the government often accused of turning a blind eye or actively participating in such campaigns.

State Media and Narratives: State-owned media outlets and government-friendly private media have played a crucial role in disseminating government propaganda. News channels and newspapers that support the government's narrative often receive preferential treatment, including advertising revenue and exclusive access to information. The use of media to promote government achievements, downplay failures, and vilify opposition parties is a common practice.

Nationalism and Unity: The use of nationalism as a propaganda tool has been particularly evident in recent years.

The government has promoted a narrative of national unity and strength, often framing opposition to government policies as unpatriotic or anti-national. This has been especially prominent in the context of conflicts with neighbouring countries, such as China and Pakistan, where the government has used nationalist rhetoric to rally public support and deflect criticism.

Global Comparisons

Globally, propaganda and media manipulation are common tactics used by both authoritarian and democratic governments. In China, state-controlled media and internet censorship ensure that only the government's narrative reaches the public. The Chinese government uses propaganda to promote its achievements, justify its policies, and suppress any dissenting voices. The portrayal of China's handling of the COVID-19 pandemic and the Hong Kong protests are examples of how the state uses media to control the narrative and maintain its authority.

Russia has perfected the use of propaganda both domestically and internationally. Domestically, the government controls major media outlets and uses them to promote pro-Kremlin narratives, discredit opposition, and foster a sense of Russian nationalism. Internationally, Russia employs state-funded media outlets like RT and Sputnik to spread its narrative, influence public opinion in other countries, and create confusion and division. The use of disinformation campaigns, particularly during elections in other countries, has become a hallmark of Russian propaganda.

In the United States and other Western democracies, propaganda is more subtle and often takes the form of political spin, advertising, and public relations campaigns. Governments use media briefings, press releases, and social media to shape public perception and promote their policies.

While there is more freedom of the press, the line between information and propaganda can become blurred, particularly during times of crisis or conflict.

Psychological Impact on Populations

The Effects of Surveillance and Censorship

The pervasive nature of surveillance and censorship has profound psychological effects on populations. The knowledge that one is being watched, monitored, or censored can lead to self-censorship, a phenomenon where individuals avoid expressing dissenting opinions or engaging in activities that could draw the attention of the authorities. This creates a climate of fear and conformity, where the free exchange of ideas is stifled, and critical thinking is discouraged.

In India, the impact of surveillance and censorship is evident in the way individuals and organizations approach sensitive topics. Journalists, activists, and ordinary citizens are increasingly wary of voicing criticism against the government or discussing controversial issues, fearing legal repercussions or social backlash. This has led to a decline in public discourse and a narrowing of the space for debate and dissent.

Globally, in countries with high levels of surveillance, like China and Russia, the psychological impact is even more pronounced. The presence of a surveillance state instils a sense of paranoia and mistrust among citizens, who are constantly aware that their actions and words are being monitored. This can lead to a homogenization of thought and behaviour, as individuals conform to avoid attracting attention or punishment.

Propaganda and its Influence on Public Perception

Propaganda works on a psychological level by shaping perceptions, beliefs, and attitudes. By consistently presenting a particular narrative, propaganda can create a sense of reality that aligns with the government's goals. Over time, repeated exposure to propaganda can lead to the internalization of state-approved narratives, making it difficult for individuals to distinguish between truth and manipulation.

In India, the use of propaganda has contributed to a polarized society, where people are often divided along ideological lines. The dissemination of biased or misleading information through media and social platforms has created echo chambers, where individuals are exposed only to views that reinforce their pre-existing beliefs. This has led to an erosion of trust in traditional media and institutions as people increasingly rely on partisan sources for information.

In countries like China, where state control over information is absolute, propaganda has been used to foster a sense of national pride and loyalty to the Communist Party. The government's narrative of economic progress, social stability, and national strength is deeply ingrained in the public consciousness, making it difficult for alternative viewpoints to gain traction. This creates a society where dissent is not only suppressed by the state but also socially discouraged by peers.

Psychological Warfare and Misinformation

Beyond shaping narratives, propaganda and disinformation can be used as tools of psychological warfare. By spreading misinformation, governments and political actors can create confusion, sow distrust, and destabilize societies. This tactic has been employed not only by authoritarian states but also in democratic contexts, where misinformation is used to influence elections, polarize public opinion, and undermine confidence in democratic institutions.

In the global context, Russia's use of disinformation campaigns to influence elections and create societal divisions in other countries is a prime example of psychological warfare. The spread of fake news and conspiracy theories during the 2016 US presidential election and the Brexit referendum in the UK demonstrated the power of misinformation to shape public perception and alter political outcomes.

In India, misinformation and fake news have become significant challenges, particularly during elections and times of social unrest. The spread of false information through social media and messaging platforms has led to real-world consequences, including violence and the breakdown of social cohesion. The government's response to misinformation has often been criticized as inadequate or politically motivated, with efforts to control the narrative sometimes exacerbating the problem.

Impact on Social Cohesion and Trust

The cumulative effect of surveillance, censorship, and propaganda is the erosion of social cohesion and trust. When people are constantly monitored, censored, and subjected to propaganda, they become less likely to trust not only the government but also each other. This breakdown of trust undermines the social fabric, leading to increased polarization, fragmentation, and social conflict.

In India, the use of surveillance, censorship, and propaganda has contributed to a climate of suspicion and division. The portrayal of certain groups as threats to national security or social order has led to the marginalization and alienation of these communities. The resulting social tensions have been exacerbated by the spread of misinformation and the manipulation of public perception, leading to a more divided society.

Globally, the psychological impact of these control mechanisms is evident in the increasing polarization and distrust in many countries. In authoritarian states like China and Russia, the lack of trust in government and social institutions is counterbalanced by fear and a sense of powerlessness. In democracies, the erosion of trust in media, political institutions, and fellow citizens poses a significant threat to democratic norms and values.

The control mechanisms of surveillance, censorship, and propaganda have become more sophisticated and pervasive in the modern era. These tools are used not only by authoritarian regimes but also by democracies facing challenges of governance and social cohesion. India, while a democracy, has employed these mechanisms in ways that raise concerns about the erosion of democratic norms and the impact on individual freedoms and social cohesion.

The psychological impact of these control mechanisms is profound, shaping public perception, behaviour, and trust. In the long term, the use of surveillance, censorship, and propaganda undermines the free exchange of ideas, fosters a climate of fear and conformity, and erodes the social fabric. As these trends continue to unfold, it is crucial for societies to find a balance between security, governance, and the protection of fundamental rights and freedoms. The global community must remain vigilant and proactive in safeguarding the principles of open and democratic societies, ensuring that the tools of modernity are used to empower rather than control.

Indian Diaspora: Cultural Integration Abroad

The Indian diaspora, one of the largest and most diverse in the world, has a significant presence across continents, influencing and being influenced by the cultures of their adopted countries. The migration of Indians abroad spans centuries, with the earliest movements occurring during the colonial period and continuing to the present day. This diaspora, estimated to be over 30 million strong, is known for its ability to adapt and integrate while preserving its cultural identity. The process of cultural integration for the Indian diaspora is complex, involving a delicate balance between maintaining cultural heritage and assimilating into the host society.

Historical Context of Indian Migration

Indian migration has a long history, beginning with ancient trade routes and continuing through various phases of colonialism and globalization. During the British colonial era, a significant number of Indians were transported as indentured labourers to work on plantations in the Caribbean, Africa, and Southeast Asia. These early migrants faced harsh conditions and were often isolated from their homeland, yet they managed to establish communities that preserved elements of Indian culture.

The post-independence period saw a different wave of migration driven by economic opportunities and educational pursuits. The 1960s and 1970s witnessed a significant movement of skilled professionals, particularly doctors, engineers, and academics, to countries such as the United States, Canada, United Kingdom, and Australia. This trend continued into the late 20th and early 21st centuries with the rise of the information technology industry, leading to a significant influx of Indian professionals into Western countries.

The Dynamics of Cultural Integration

Cultural integration for the Indian diaspora involves navigating a complex landscape of identity, tradition, and adaptation. Indians abroad have often had to reconcile the cultural values and practices of their homeland with those of the host country. This process varies significantly depending on factors such as the country of residence, the migrant's socioeconomic status, and the level of community support available.

One of the key aspects of cultural integration is the retention and transmission of cultural heritage. The Indian diaspora has been remarkably successful in maintaining its cultural identity through various means. Indian communities abroad celebrate festivals such as Diwali, Holi, Eid, and Vaisakhi with great enthusiasm, providing a sense of continuity and belonging. Religious practices and institutions, including Hindu temples, Sikh gurdwaras, and Islamic mosques, serve as focal points for cultural and spiritual life, helping to preserve traditional values and customs.

Language plays a crucial role in cultural retention. Many members of the Indian diaspora make efforts to teach their native languages, such as Hindi, Tamil, Punjabi, Gujarati, and Bengali, to the younger generation. Cultural organizations and community centres often offer classes in Indian languages, dance, music, and other cultural arts, fostering a sense of pride and identity among the diaspora.

Assimilation and Adaptation

While the Indian diaspora places a strong emphasis on cultural preservation, it also engages in processes of assimilation and adaptation. This involves adopting elements of the host culture, such as language, lifestyle, and social norms, while simultaneously retaining a distinct cultural identity.

Assimilation is often seen in areas such as education, employment, and social interaction, where members of the diaspora engage with the broader society and contribute to its diversity.

In countries like United States, Canada, and United Kingdom, the Indian diaspora has been successful in integrating into the professional and academic spheres. Indian Americans, for instance, are one of the most educated and economically successful immigrant groups in the United States, with a strong presence in fields such as technology, medicine, and academia. This success has facilitated greater acceptance and inclusion within mainstream society, allowing Indians to navigate multiple cultural identities with relative ease.

However, the process of assimilation can also be challenging, particularly for the first generation of migrants, who may experience cultural dissonance and identity conflicts. Balancing the expectations of their cultural heritage with the demands of the host society can lead to feelings of alienation and struggle. The second and subsequent generations, who grow up in the host country, often experience a different set of challenges as they negotiate their identity between their parents' culture and the culture they are raised in.

Cultural Exchange and Influence

The Indian diaspora has not only integrated into host societies but has also had a significant cultural impact on them. Indian culture, in its various forms, has become an integral part of the cultural mosaic in many countries. Indian cuisine, for example, has gained widespread popularity around the world, with dishes like curry, biryani, and samosas becoming household names. Indian restaurants, food festivals, and cooking shows have introduced global audiences to the rich and diverse culinary traditions of India.

The influence of Indian culture extends to other domains, such as music, dance, and cinema. Bollywood, India's prolific film industry, has a massive global following, with Indian movies being watched by audiences in countries as diverse as the United States, United Kingdom, Nigeria, and Russia. Indian classical music and dance forms, such as Bharatanatyam, Kathak, and Carnatic music, have also found appreciative audiences abroad, with many practitioners and students of these arts hailing from non-Indian backgrounds.

Yoga and meditation, rooted in ancient Indian traditions, have become global phenomena, embraced by people of all cultures as means of physical fitness and spiritual well-being. The Indian diaspora has played a pivotal role in popularizing these practices, establishing yoga studios, wellness centres, and spiritual retreats around the world.

The cultural exchange facilitated by the Indian diaspora has enriched host societies, promoting diversity and fostering greater understanding and appreciation of different cultural traditions. This exchange is a two-way process, as the diaspora also adopts and adapts elements of the host culture, creating a dynamic interplay between cultures.

Challenges and Identity Politics

Despite the success of the Indian diaspora in integrating and influencing host societies, challenges remain. Issues of racism, discrimination, and identity politics continue to affect the diaspora, particularly in countries where immigration and cultural diversity are contentious topics. The experience of the Indian diaspora is shaped by the broader social and political context of the host country, which can vary significantly in terms of attitudes towards multiculturalism and immigration.

In some countries, the Indian diaspora has faced xenophobia and stereotyping, with individuals being subjected to prejudice based on their ethnicity, religion, or nationality. The post-9/11 environment, for example, saw an increase in anti-Asian sentiment and hate crimes in Western countries, affecting not only Indians but also other South Asian and Middle Eastern communities. Such experiences can create a sense of vulnerability and marginalization, complicating the process of integration.

Identity politics also plays a role in shaping the experiences of the Indian diaspora. The question of identity – whether to identify primarily with the host country, the country of origin, or both – can be a source of tension and debate within the diaspora. This is particularly evident among the younger generation, who may feel caught between the cultural expectations of their parents and their own desire to assimilate into the mainstream culture of the host country.

The Role of Transnational Networks

Transnational networks and connections play a crucial role in the cultural integration of the Indian diaspora. Advances in communication technology and increased global mobility have made it easier for diaspora communities to maintain ties with their homeland and with other Indian communities around the world. These connections facilitate the exchange of cultural practices, ideas, and resources, creating a global Indian identity that transcends national boundaries.

Diaspora organizations, cultural associations, and online platforms provide spaces for Indians abroad to connect, share experiences, and celebrate their cultural heritage. These networks also play a role in advocacy and community support, addressing issues such as immigration, education, and social integration. The Indian government has recognized the importance of the diaspora and has established initiatives to engage with and support Indians abroad, including the Pravasi Bharatiya Divas (Non-Resident Indian Day) and the Overseas Citizen of India (OCI) program.

The Indian diaspora represents a unique example of cultural integration, characterized by its ability to maintain a strong cultural identity while adapting to and influencing the societies it inhabits. This integration is a dynamic process that involves navigating the complexities of identity, tradition, and adaptation in a multicultural world.

As the Indian diaspora continues to grow and evolve, it will play an increasingly important role in shaping the cultural and social dynamics of the 21st century. Its ability to navigate the complexities of cultural integration offers valuable insights into the broader processes of globalization, migration, and multiculturalism, highlighting the importance of diversity, tolerance, and cross-cultural exchange in an interconnected world.

PART 3

RESISTANCE AND REVOLUTION

Chapter 8
Historical Revolutions

Resistance and revolution are fundamental responses to oppression and injustice, often emerging in societies where people's rights and freedoms are severely restricted. Resistance can take many forms, from non-violent protests, civil disobedience, and strikes to the formation of underground movements. It embodies the collective will of the people to challenge authority, fight against abuses of power, and demand change.

When resistance gains momentum, it can lead to revolution – a radical shift aimed at overthrowing an oppressive regime and transforming the political and social order. Revolutions are driven by the pursuit of justice, equality, and liberation, often requiring great sacrifices from those involved. They represent a powerful force for societal change, reshaping the balance of power and striving to replace despotism with systems that honour human dignity and freedom.

Major Revolutions and Their Causes

India's history, much like global history, is rich with movements of resistance and revolution that have shaped its society and political landscape. From ancient rebellions against oppressive regimes to the struggle for independence from British colonial rule, India has witnessed several pivotal moments that reflect the broader dynamics of revolutionary change. Globally, revolutions like the American, French, Russian, and Chinese revolutions have similarly redefined power structures and altered the course of nations. This chapter examines significant revolutions and movements in Indian history and compares them to major global revolutions, exploring their causes and lasting impact.

The Indian Rebellion of 1857

Causes: The Indian Rebellion of 1857, also known as the First War of Independence, was a major uprising against the British East India Company's rule. The rebellion's causes were multifaceted, encompassing economic exploitation, social and religious grievances, and political disenfranchisement. The British policies of economic exploitation, including heavy taxation and the introduction of the exploitative Zamindari system, impoverished Indian peasants and artisans. Moreover, British disregard for Indian cultural and religious practices, such as the introduction of Enfield rifles rumoured to be greased with cow and pig fat, inflamed religious sentiments among Hindu and Muslim soldiers (sepoys). The annexation of Indian states through the Doctrine of Lapse further fueled resentment among the Indian princes and ruling class.

The rebellion was not merely a spontaneous outburst but rather a culmination of decades of oppressive rule and systemic exploitation. The immediate spark may have been the issue of the cartridges, but the underlying grievances of poverty, forced westernization, and systematic disrespect towards traditional authority were the real fuel for the revolt.

The Catalysts

Economic Exploitation: The imposition of high taxes, coupled with the British policy of flooding the Indian market with British goods while undermining Indian industries, led to widespread economic ruin. Artisans and weavers, in particular, suffered from policies that favoured British manufactured goods.

Religious and Cultural Insensitivity: The introduction of social reforms by the British was perceived as an attempt to undermine traditional religious beliefs. The rumours about the rifle cartridges, whether true or not, played into existing fears that the British sought to Christianize India.

Political Disenfranchisement: The Doctrine of Lapse, which allowed the British to annex states with no male heir, directly threatened Indian rulers. Many saw this as a blatant attempt by the British to destroy Indian sovereignty.

Global Comparison: Similar to the American Revolution (1775-1783), where economic exploitation and lack of representation ('no taxation without representation') drove the colonies to revolt against British rule, the Indian Rebellion of 1857 also reflected a deep-seated resentment against exploitative colonial policies and political disenfranchisement. Both revolutions were driven by a shared desire for autonomy and a rejection of foreign rule that oppressed local populations.

The Indian Independence Movement (1857-1947)

Causes: The Indian Independence Movement was a prolonged struggle against British colonial rule, marked by a series of movements, uprisings, and mass mobilizations. The causes were rooted in the economic, social, and political exploitation of India by the British Empire. The systematic drain of wealth, the imposition of British economic policies that favoured British industries at the expense of Indian artisans and farmers, and the denial of political and civil rights to Indians led to growing discontent. The introduction of Western education and ideas of liberty and self-governance further fueled the desire for independence. Pivotal events such as the partition of Bengal in 1905, the Jallianwala Bagh massacre in 1919, and the repressive Rowlatt Act galvanized public sentiment against British rule.

The movement evolved from sporadic revolts to a mass civil disobedience campaign under leaders like Mahatma Gandhi, whose philosophy of non-violent resistance inspired millions to fight for their freedom. The Indian National Congress became the political platform that unified diverse groups under a single banner for independence.

The Catalysts

Economic Exploitation: The deindustrialization of India and the exploitation of its resources for the benefit of the British economy led to widespread poverty and resentment. Indian farmers were forced into cash crop cultivation, which resulted in famines and food shortages, while profits from Indian resources were siphoned off to England.

Social and Cultural Suppression: British attempts to impose cultural norms, such as promoting English as the language of administration and education, and disregarding Indian customs, led to a loss of cultural heritage and identity. It also led to the alienation of the educated Indian middle class, who were taught ideals of democracy but denied political participation.

Political Oppression: The lack of political representation, coupled with harsh measures like the Rowlatt Act (which allowed the government to imprison individuals without trial) and the brutality of incidents like the Jallianwala Bagh massacre, further fueled the demand for self-rule.

Global Comparison: The French Revolution (1789-1799), driven by widespread economic hardship, social inequality, and political mismanagement, shared many similarities with the Indian struggle. Both revolutions were fueled by an unyielding demand for political representation and the dismantling of oppressive structures. Just as the French Revolution sought to overthrow the monarchy and establish equality, the Indian Independence Movement aimed to dismantle British imperial rule and establish sovereignty.

Peasant and Tribal Movements

Causes: India's history is replete with peasant and tribal uprisings against oppressive landlords, colonial policies, and exploitative economic systems. Movements such as the Indigo Rebellion (1859-60) in Bengal, the Santhal Rebellion (1855-56) in present-day Jharkhand, and the Telangana Rebellion (1946-51) in Andhra Pradesh were driven by the exploitation of peasants and tribal communities by landlords and colonial authorities. Economic exploitation included excessive taxation, forced cultivation of cash crops, and the confiscation of land. Tribal movements also responded to the encroachment on their land and the destruction of traditional ways of life.

These movements highlighted the widespread discontent among marginalized communities that were largely ignored by mainstream nationalist politics. The tribal and peasant uprisings often emerged in remote areas where state control was weaker, and traditional ways of life were severely disrupted by colonial and feudal practices.

The Catalysts:

Land and Resource Exploitation: Imposed land revenue systems, such as the Permanent Settlement, led to landlords exploiting peasants to meet high revenue demands. In many tribal areas, British policies led to the displacement of indigenous people from their ancestral lands.

Cultural and Social Suppression: Encroachment on tribal lands and the imposition of foreign cultural practices threatened traditional livelihoods and identities. Tribal leaders, such as Birsa Munda, arose to challenge these impositions and restore traditional social orders.

Lack of Legal and Political Recourse: The absence of legal protections and political representation for peasants and tribals exacerbated their grievances, leaving violent rebellion as one of the few available options for resisting exploitation.

Global Comparison: The Russian Revolution (1917) similarly involved mass discontent among peasants and workers who faced economic exploitation and social injustice. In both Russia and India, the failure to address these grievances led to widespread rebellion against oppressive authorities. The Russian peasants, like their Indian counterparts, revolted against a feudal system that kept them in perpetual poverty.

Role of Leadership and Ideology

Leadership and ideology have been central to the success and direction of revolutionary movements. Leaders who could articulate the aspirations of the masses and offer a vision for a better future played crucial roles in mobilizing and sustaining revolutionary efforts. The ideologies underpinning these movements provided a framework for understanding the causes of oppression and envisioning a just society.

Leadership in Revolutions

Mangal Pandey and the 1857 Rebellion

Mangal Pandey is often celebrated as one of the first leaders of the Indian Rebellion of 1857. His defiance against the use of Enfield rifle cartridges, believed to be greased with cow and pig fat, ignited rebellion among the sepoys. Pandey's act of resistance became a symbol of the larger struggle against British rule. Though the rebellion lacked unified leadership, figures like Rani Lakshmibai of Jhansi, Tantia Tope, and Bahadur Shah Zafar played significant roles in leading their respective forces.

Mahatma Gandhi and the Independence Movement

Mahatma Gandhi's leadership transformed the Indian independence struggle into a mass movement. His philosophy of nonviolent resistance (Satyagraha) and civil disobedience inspired millions to participate in the struggle for freedom. Gandhi's ability to mobilize diverse sections of Indian society – including peasants, workers, and women – and his emphasis on moral principles made him a unifying figure. His leadership during key events like the Non-Cooperation Movement, the

Salt March, and the Quit India Movement galvanized public support for independence.

Global Comparison

Gandhi's leadership can be compared to George Washington's role in the American Revolution. Both leaders were instrumental in inspiring and uniting their people against a common colonial oppressor, using both strategy and ideology to galvanize support. Just as Washington's leadership in the Continental Army helped secure American independence, Gandhi's leadership in non-violent resistance was crucial in securing Indian freedom.

Vladimir Lenin and the Russian Revolution: Lenin was the ideological and strategic mastermind behind the Bolshevik Revolution. His leadership was marked by his ability to mobilize the masses and articulate a clear vision for a socialist state. Lenin's adaptation of Marxist theory to Russia's unique context, including the emphasis on a vanguard party, proved decisive in overthrowing the provisional government and establishing a communist regime.

The Role of Ideology

Gandhian Philosophy

Gandhi's ideology was rooted in non-violence (ahimsa), truth (satya), and self-reliance (swadeshi). His philosophy emphasized peaceful resistance and individual moral responsibility, resonating with the Indian populace and providing a moral framework for the independence movement. Gandhi's vision of a self-sufficient, decentralized economy and a society free from caste discrimination laid the foundation for a new social order.

Marxism and Leninism

Leninism adapted Marxist ideology to the Russian context, emphasizing the need for a disciplined vanguard party to lead the revolution and the use of revolutionary violence to seize power. The concept of the 'dictatorship of the proletariat' as a transitional phase toward a classless society became a cornerstone of Soviet governance.

Global Comparison

Similar ideological currents can be found in Maoism during the Chinese Revolution, where Mao adapted Marxist theory to emphasize the role of the peasantry in the revolution. The emphasis on continuous struggle to prevent new forms of oppression and the mobilization of the masses for socialist goals mirrored the revolutionary zeal in both Russia and India.

Outcomes and Lessons Learned

The revolutionary movements and struggles in India, as well as globally, have had profound impacts on their respective nations' political, social, and economic landscapes. While some revolutions succeeded in achieving their initial goals, others gave rise to new challenges and even new forms of oppression.

Indian Independence Movement

The movement culminated in the end of nearly 200 years of British colonial rule and the establishment of an independent India in 1947. However, the partition of India and Pakistan led to one of the largest mass migrations in history and widespread communal violence. The movement fostered a sense of national identity and unity among India's diverse peoples, and its legacy is reflected in the Indian Constitution, which enshrines democracy, secularism, and social justice.

Global Comparison

Similar to the American Revolution, which led to the establishment of an independent nation founded on democratic principles, the Indian independence movement resulted in the creation of a democratic republic. Both nations faced challenges in reconciling their revolutionary ideals with existing social inequalities – America struggled with slavery and the rights of indigenous peoples, while India faced challenges related to caste and communalism.

Russian Revolution

The Russian Revolution resulted in the overthrow of the autocratic Romanov dynasty and led to the establishment of the Soviet Union – the world's first socialist state. The revolution resulted in radical social and economic changes, but also led to a repressive regime marked by political purges and forced collectivization. The long-term impact included the spread of communist ideology and the Cold War, which shaped global politics for decades.

Lessons Learned

Mass Mobilization as a Tool for Change: Both India and global revolutions, like those in France and America, demonstrate the power of mass mobilization. The Indian Independence Movement succeeded in involving people across caste, religion, and regional lines, illustrating that inclusive and grassroot approaches are critical for sustaining revolutionary momentum.

Ideological Diversity and Unity: India's revolutionary movements encompassed a diversity of ideologies – from Gandhi's non-violence to militant nationalism. This diversity allowed multiple forms of resistance but also presented challenges for unity, similar to the ideological struggles seen during the French Revolution between the Girondins and Jacobins, where competing visions of governance led to internal conflicts and eventual radicalization.

Post-Revolution Reconstruction: The challenges of building new institutions after revolutions have been evident across different contexts. In India, the transition involved establishing democratic institutions, a challenge paralleled by the United States, which faced the task of creating a stable constitutional framework. In Russia and China, the failure to create inclusive systems after the revolutions led to authoritarian regimes.

Global Influence and External Factors: The success or challenges faced by revolutionary movements are often influenced by international factors. The American Revolution benefited from French support, while the Russian Revolution occurred amidst World War I, highlighting how external dynamics can shape revolutionary outcomes. In India, the weakening of the British Empire due to World War II played a significant role in accelerating the push for independence.

India's history of resistance and revolution is a testament to the resilience and determination of its people. The major revolutions and movements in India, from the Rebellion of 1857 to the Independence Movement, reflect similar dynamics seen in global revolutions like those in America, France, Russia, and China. The role of leadership and ideology has been crucial in shaping the direction and outcomes of these struggles for freedom and justice.

The outcomes of revolutionary movements have been significant, leading to the establishment of new political orders, albeit with challenges of social and economic justice remaining. The lessons from India's revolutionary history and global revolutions offer valuable insights into the dynamics of resistance, the complexities of post-revolution reconstruction, and the importance of inclusive and sustained efforts to achieve social change.

Revolutions are moments of profound transformation driven by the desire for a more just and equitable society. Yet, they often face the dual challenge of achieving their ideals while navigating the practical realities of governance and reconstruction. The spirit of resistance and the pursuit of justice remain enduring legacies in the ongoing quest for a more equitable world, reminding us that the journey of revolution is never truly complete but is a continuing struggle for a better society.

Chapter 9
Modern Resistance Movements

Modern resistance movements have evolved in response to the complexities of the contemporary world, encompassing a range of issues such as civil rights, social justice, environmental activism, and digital privacy. These movements arise from systemic inequalities, state repression, and the desire for greater freedom and autonomy. In an interconnected global landscape, resistance has become more visible, sophisticated, and dynamic. This chapter explores the nature of modern resistance movements with a focus on civil rights movements globally, protests and uprisings in India, and the role of technology in shaping these movements.

Civil Rights Movements

Civil rights movements have been pivotal in challenging systemic discrimination and advocating for the equal treatment of marginalized communities. These movements have spanned across continents, addressing issues such as racial inequality, gender discrimination, LGBTQ+ rights, and more. Despite the differences in the specific sociopolitical contexts in which they arise, these movements share common themes of demanding dignity, justice, and equality.

The Civil Rights Movement in the United States

Background and Causes: The Civil Rights Movement in the United States (1950s-1960s) was a monumental struggle against racial segregation and discrimination. African Americans had long been subjected to systemic racism, particularly in the Southern states, where Jim Crow laws enforced segregation in public spaces, education, and employment. The movement emerged as a response to the deep-rooted injustices faced by African Americans, including disenfranchisement, economic inequality, and racial violence.

Key Events and Leadership

Montgomery Bus Boycott (1955-56): Sparked by Rosa Parks' refusal to give up her seat to a white person, this year-long boycott became a powerful protest against racial segregation in public transportation.

March on Washington (1963): A historic rally where Martin Luther King Jr. delivered his iconic "I Have a Dream" speech, calling for an end to racism and the realization of civil and economic rights for African Americans.

Civil Rights Act (1964) and Voting Rights Act (1965): These landmark legislations ended segregation in public places and banned discriminatory voting practices, marking significant victories for the movement.

Impact and Legacy: The Civil Rights Movement transformed American society by challenging institutionalized racism and securing legal protections for African Americans. It laid the groundwork for subsequent movements advocating for the rights of other marginalized groups, including women, LGBTQ+ individuals, and immigrants. The movement's emphasis on non-violent protest and civil disobedience has influenced global resistance movements, highlighting the power of peaceful activism.

Anti-Apartheid Movement in South Africa

Background and Causes: The Anti-Apartheid Movement was a global campaign against South Africa's apartheid system, a regime of racial segregation and discrimination enforced by the government from 1948 to 1994. Under apartheid, the white minority government imposed strict racial laws, denying the Black majority basic human rights, including political representation, freedom of movement, and access to quality education and healthcare.

Key Events and Leadership

Sharpeville Massacre (1960): A turning point in the struggle against apartheid, where police opened fire on peaceful protesters, killing 69 people. This event drew international condemnation and intensified resistance efforts.

Nelson Mandela and the African National Congress (ANC): Nelson Mandela became the face of the anti-apartheid struggle, advocating for armed resistance after peaceful efforts were met with violent repression. Despite his imprisonment for 27 years, Mandela's resilience became a symbol of the fight for freedom and equality.

International Sanctions and Boycotts: Global solidarity played a crucial role in dismantling apartheid, with countries imposing economic sanctions and boycotts against South Africa, pressuring the government to dismantle the apartheid system.

Impact and Legacy: The Anti-Apartheid Movement succeeded in ending institutionalized racial discrimination, leading to the establishment of a democratic South Africa in 1994 with Nelson Mandela as its first Black president. The movement's legacy endures in its lessons on the power of international solidarity, the importance of resilience in the face of oppression, and the possibility of reconciliation and nation-building after deep societal divisions.

Women's Rights Movements

Background and Causes: Women's rights movements have been a global phenomenon, advocating for gender equality and challenging patriarchal structures that marginalize women. These movements have sought to address issues such as the right to vote, equal pay, reproductive rights, and protection against gender-based violence.

Key Events and Leadership

Suffrage Movement: The fight for women's right to vote was a major early victory for women's rights movements in many countries, including the United States and the United Kingdom. Leaders like Susan B. Anthony, Emmeline Pankhurst, and others were instrumental in securing this fundamental right.

#MeToo Movement: In recent years, the #MeToo movement has gained global traction, highlighting the pervasive issue of sexual harassment and assault. It has empowered women to speak out against abuse and has brought about significant changes in social attitudes and policies regarding gender-based violence.

Impact and Legacy: Women's rights movements have led to substantial legal and societal changes, including the right to vote, gender equality in the workplace, and greater awareness of gender-based violence. These movements continue to evolve, addressing ongoing issues such as reproductive rights, pay equity, and the representation of women in leadership positions.

LGBTQ+ Rights Movements

Background and Causes: LGBTQ+ rights movements have sought to challenge societal norms and legal frameworks that discriminate against individuals based on their sexual orientation or gender identity. These movements have addressed issues such as criminalization, discrimination, and the right to marriage and family life.

Key Events and Leadership

Stonewall Riots (1969): The Stonewall Riots in New York City are often regarded as the catalyst for the modern LGBTQ+ rights movement. The riots were a response to police raids on the Stonewall Inn, a gay bar, and they galvanized the community to demand equal rights and recognition.

Marriage Equality: The fight for marriage equality has been a significant focus of LGBTQ+ movements worldwide, resulting in the legalization of same-sex marriage in numerous countries, including the United States, Canada, and many European nations.

Impact and Legacy: LGBTQ+ rights movements have achieved significant milestones, including the decriminalization of homosexuality in many countries, legal recognition of same-sex marriages, and increased social acceptance. However, these movements continue to face challenges, particularly in regions where LGBTQ+ individuals are still subject to legal and societal discrimination.

Protests and Uprisings in India

India has a rich history of protests and uprisings, reflecting the country's diverse and complex social fabric. These movements have often been driven by the desire to address social injustices, challenge state policies, or advocate for the rights of marginalized communities. In recent years, India has witnessed a surge in protests addressing a range of issues, from economic inequality to religious intolerance.

Anti-Corruption Movement (2011)

Background and Causes: The Anti-Corruption Movement of 2011 was sparked by widespread public frustration with government corruption and lack of accountability. The movement was catalyzed by a series of high-profile corruption scandals, including the 2G spectrum scam and the Commonwealth Games scam, which exposed the extent of corruption at the highest levels of government.

Key Events and Leadership

Anna Hazare and the Jan Lokpal Bill: Social activist Anna Hazare became the face of the movement, advocating for the implementation of the Jan Lokpal Bill, a proposed anti-corruption law that aimed to create an independent body to investigate and prosecute corrupt officials. Hazare's hunger strike at Jantar Mantar in New Delhi attracted massive public support and media attention.

Public Mobilization: The movement saw widespread participation from people across India, including the middle class, students, and professionals. The use of social media and digital platforms played a significant role in mobilizing support and coordinating protests.

Impact and Legacy: The Anti-Corruption Movement succeeded in raising public awareness about the issue of corruption and pressuring the government to pass the Lokpal and Lokayuktas Act in 2013. Although the effectiveness of the law has been debated, the movement demonstrated the power of collective action and the potential for civil society to influence government policy. It also marked a significant moment in India's democratic discourse, highlighting the demand for greater transparency and accountability.

Nirbhaya Movement (2012-13)

Background and Causes: The Nirbhaya Movement was triggered by the brutal gang rape and murder of a young woman in Delhi in December 2012. The incident shocked the nation and sparked widespread outrage, bringing to the forefront the issue of gender-based violence and the safety of women in India. The movement was named 'Nirbhaya' (meaning 'fearless') in honour of the victim, whose plight became a symbol of the broader struggle against sexual violence.

Key Events and Public Response

Mass Protests: The incident led to massive protests across India, particularly in Delhi, where thousands of people took to the streets to demand justice for the victim and stricter laws to protect women. The protests were marked by candlelight vigils, marches, and demonstrations, reflecting the public's deep anger and demand for change.

Legal Reforms: In response to the public outcry, the Indian government set up the Justice Verma Committee to review existing laws on sexual violence. The committee's recommendations led to significant legal reforms, including the Criminal Law (Amendment) Act of 2013, which expanded the definition of sexual assault, increased penalties for offenders, and established new procedures for the protection of women's rights.

Impact and Legacy: The Nirbhaya Movement brought about a societal awakening regarding the prevalence of sexual violence in India and the need for systemic change. It resulted in stricter laws and greater public awareness about women's rights and safety. However, the persistence of gender-based violence and the challenges in implementing these laws highlight the ongoing struggle for gender equality and justice in India.

Farmer Protests (2020-21)

Background and Causes: The Farmer Protests of 2020-21 were sparked by the Indian government's introduction of three agricultural laws aimed at liberalizing the farming sector. The laws were intended to allow farmers to sell their produce outside of state-regulated markets (mandis), ostensibly to provide greater market access and improve efficiency. However, many farmers feared that these laws would lead to the dismantling of the minimum support price (MSP) system and expose them to exploitation by large corporations.

Key Events and Mobilization

Mass Protests and Encampments: Farmers from Punjab, Haryana, and other states marched to Delhi, setting up large encampments on the borders of the city. The protests were marked by sit-ins, tractor rallies, and sustained demonstrations, with farmers demanding the repeal of the laws.

National and International Solidarity: The protests garnered widespread support from across India and from the Indian diaspora worldwide. Solidarity rallies were held in various countries, and the movement received significant attention on social media and international news outlets.

Impact and Legacy: The Farmer Protests highlighted the challenges faced by India's agricultural sector and the deep-seated concerns of farmers regarding market reforms. After more than a year of protests, the Indian government announced the repeal of the three farm laws in November 2021, marking a significant victory for the movement. The protests underscored the power of grassroots mobilization and the importance of dialogue and negotiation in addressing contentious policy issues.

Citizenship Amendment Act (CAA) Protests (2019-20)

Background and Causes: The Citizenship Amendment Act (CAA) of 2019, which sought to provide a path to citizenship for non-Muslim immigrants from neighbouring countries, sparked widespread protests across India. Critics argued that the law was discriminatory as it excluded Muslims and undermined the secular principles enshrined in the Indian Constitution. The protests were also fueled by concerns about the potential implementation of the National Register of Citizens (NRC), which many feared could lead to the disenfranchisement of Muslim citizens.

Key Events and Public Response

Nationwide Protests: The CAA protests saw participation from a diverse cross-section of Indian society, including students, activists, intellectuals, and ordinary citizens. Major protests were held in cities like Delhi, Mumbai, Kolkata, and Bangalore, with sit-ins, marches, and demonstrations calling for the repeal of the law.

Shaheen Bagh and Symbolic Resistance: The protest at Shaheen Bagh in Delhi became a symbolic centre of the movement, where predominantly Muslim women led a peaceful sit-in for several months. The protest gained widespread attention for its inclusive and non-violent nature, with participants from different communities coming together to express solidarity.

Impact and Legacy: The CAA protests brought attention to the contentious issue of citizenship and the rising tide of majoritarian politics in India. While the government did not repeal the law, the protests sparked a national debate on the principles of secularism, inclusivity, and the rights of minorities. The movement also highlighted the resilience and agency of civil society in challenging state policies perceived as unjust.

Role of Technology in Modern Resistance

In the digital age, technology has become an indispensable tool for modern resistance movements. The advent of the internet, social media, and mobile communication has transformed the way movements are organized, mobilized, and disseminated.

Technology has enabled activists to bypass traditional media, reach a global audience, and create networks of solidarity that transcend geographical boundaries.

Digital Mobilization and Social Media

Organizing and Coordinating Protests: Social media platforms like Facebook, Twitter, and Instagram have played a crucial role in organizing and coordinating protests. Activists use these platforms to share information, plan events, and mobilize supporters. Hashtags and viral posts can quickly spread awareness and galvanize public support, as seen in movements like #BlackLivesMatter and #MeToo. In India, the Farmer Protests and CAA protests used social media to coordinate actions and disseminate information despite attempts at censorship and misinformation.

Amplifying Voices and Counter-Narratives: Social media has provided a platform for marginalized voices and counter-narratives that are often ignored or suppressed by mainstream media. Activists can share personal stories, document human rights abuses, and challenge dominant discourses. The use of live streaming and citizen journalism has enabled real-time documentation of protests and state responses, providing a powerful tool for accountability and raising international awareness.

Challenges and Limitations of Digital Activism

Censorship and Surveillance: Governments have increasingly recognized the power of digital activism and have responded with measures to control and monitor online spaces. Internet shutdowns, social media censorship, and surveillance of digital communications are commonly used to stifle dissent and disrupt protests. In India, internet shutdowns have been employed during protests, particularly in regions like Kashmir, to limit the spread of information and prevent mobilization.

Misinformation and Digital Manipulation: The same digital platforms that facilitate activism can also be used to spread misinformation and manipulate public opinion. The proliferation of fake news, propaganda, and online trolling can create confusion, polarize society, and undermine the credibility of resistance movements. Activists must navigate the challenges of combating misinformation and ensuring the authenticity and integrity of their digital campaigns.

Global Solidarity and Digital Advocacy

Building International Support: Technology has enabled resistance movements to build international support and solidarity. Activists can connect with global networks, share their struggles, and garner support from international organizations, human rights groups, and the diaspora. The global attention on the Anti-Apartheid Movement, the Hong Kong protests, and the Farmer Protests in India demonstrates how digital advocacy can amplify local issues to a global audience.

Online Campaigns and Digital Petitions: Online campaigns and digital petitions have become effective tools for raising awareness and pressuring governments and institutions to take action. Platforms like Change.org and Avaaz allow individuals to participate in global advocacy efforts, lending their voices to causes ranging from environmental protection to human rights.

These digital tools have democratized activism, making it more accessible and participatory.

Modern resistance movements have adapted to the complexities of the contemporary world, employing diverse strategies to challenge injustice, demand rights, and advocate for change. Civil rights movements globally have made significant strides in advancing the rights of marginalized communities, while protests and uprisings in India have highlighted the ongoing struggle for justice and equality within the nation's diverse social fabric. The role of technology in modern resistance has been transformative, enabling new forms of organization, communication, and advocacy.

However, these movements also face significant challenges, including state repression, censorship, and the manipulation of digital spaces. As technology continues to evolve, so too will the strategies and methods of resistance. The global and interconnected nature of modern resistance movements underscores the importance of solidarity, dialogue, and the ongoing pursuit of a more just and equitable world.

Chapter 10
The Role of International Organizations and Human Rights

The struggle for human rights has been a central concern of international organizations and civil society for decades. As global awareness of human rights issues has grown, international organizations such as the UN and various NGOs have played pivotal roles in advocating for and protecting these rights. Their efforts range from setting international standards to on-the-ground interventions in situations of conflict and human rights abuses. This chapter explores the role of international organizations in the promotion and protection of human rights, focusing on the contributions of the United Nations, the impact of NGOs, and case studies of international intervention in human rights crises.

United Nations and Human Rights

The United Nations has been at the forefront of the global human rights movement since its inception in 1945. One of its foundational objectives is 'to reaffirm faith in fundamental human rights, in the dignity and worth of the human person, in the equal rights of men and women'. Over the years, the UN has developed a comprehensive framework for the promotion and protection of human rights, encompassing a wide range of activities, including standard-setting, monitoring, and intervention.

Universal Declaration of Human Rights

Background and Significance: Adopted by the UN General Assembly in 1948, the Universal Declaration of Human Rights (UDHR) is a milestone document that enshrines the fundamental rights and freedoms to which all human beings are entitled. The UDHR was a response to the atrocities of World War II and represented a commitment by the international community to prevent such violations from occurring again. It outlines a broad spectrum of rights, including civil, political, economic, social, and cultural rights, setting a universal standard for human dignity.

Key Provisions Civil and Political Rights: These include the right to life, liberty, and security of person (Article 3); freedom from torture and degrading treatment (Article 5); and the right to a fair trial (Article 10).

Economic, Social, and Cultural Rights: These encompass the right to work and to just and favourable conditions of employment (Article 23); the right to an adequate standard of living, including food, clothing, housing, and medical care (Article 25); and the right to education (Article 26).

Impact and Legacy: The UDHR has had a profound influence on international law and human rights practice. It serves as the foundation for numerous international treaties, regional human rights instruments, and national constitutions. Although the UDHR itself is not legally binding, it has achieved the status of customary international law, meaning that its principles are considered universally applicable and binding on all states.

International Human Rights Treaties

Following the adoption of the UDHR, the United Nations developed a series of legally binding treaties to further articulate and enforce human rights standards. These treaties have been ratified by a majority of the world's nations and serve as the cornerstone of international human rights law.

Key Treaties and Their Provisions

International Covenant on Civil and Political Rights (ICCPR) (1966): The ICCPR commits its parties to respect the civil and political rights of individuals, including the right to freedom of speech, the right to assembly, and the right to a fair trial. It also establishes the Human Rights Committee, which monitors the implementation of the Covenant.

International Covenant on Economic, Social and Cultural Rights (ICESCR) (1966): The ICESCR focuses on the realization of economic, social, and cultural rights, such as the right to work, the right to education, and the right to an adequate standard of living. The Committee on Economic, Social and Cultural Rights oversees its implementation.

Convention on the Elimination of All Forms of Discrimination Against Women (CEDAW) (1979): CEDAW aims to eliminate discrimination against women in all forms and to ensure women's equal rights in areas such as education, employment, and healthcare.

Convention on the Rights of the Child (CRC) (1989): The CRC recognizes the rights of children, including the right to protection from exploitation, the right to education, and the right to participate in family, cultural, and social life.

Monitoring and Enforcement Mechanisms: These treaties are monitored by committees of independent experts who review reports submitted by state parties and issue recommendations. Some treaties, like the ICCPR, allow individuals to submit complaints if they believe their rights have been violated, providing an additional layer of accountability.

UN Human Rights Bodies

The United Nations has established various bodies and mechanisms to promote and protect human rights, including the Human Rights Council, the Office of the High Commissioner for Human Rights (OHCHR), and the Universal Periodic Review (UPR).

Human Rights Council: The Human Rights Council, established in 2006, is an intergovernmental body responsible for strengthening the promotion and protection of human rights around the globe. It addresses situations of human rights violations and makes recommendations to member states. The Council's work includes the Universal Periodic Review, a process in which the human rights record of every UN member state is reviewed and assessed.

Office of the High Commissioner for Human Rights (OHCHR): The OHCHR leads the UN's human rights efforts and works to ensure the universal enjoyment of human rights. It provides technical assistance to states, monitors and reports on human rights situations, and engages in advocacy to address violations. The OHCHR plays a critical role in supporting the implementation of international human rights standards at the national level.

Special Procedures: The Human Rights Council has established a system of special procedures, which includes independent experts, special rapporteurs, and working groups. These mechanisms investigate and report on specific human rights issues or country situations, providing valuable insights and recommendations. Special rapporteurs, for example, are appointed to focus on thematic issues such as torture, freedom of expression, and the right to health.

NGOs and their Impact

NGOs have become integral to the global human rights movement. They operate at both the grassroots and international levels, advocating for human rights, providing support to victims, and holding governments accountable for violations. NGOs often work in partnership with international organizations, including the United Nations, to advance human rights agendas and influence policy.

Advocacy and Awareness

NGOs play a crucial role in raising awareness about human rights issues and advocating for change. They engage in public campaigns, lobbying, and the dissemination of information to educate the public and influence policymakers. NGOs such as Amnesty International, Human Rights Watch, and the International Federation for Human Rights (FIDH) have been at the forefront of global advocacy efforts.

Amnesty International

Founded in 1961, Amnesty International is one of the world's most prominent human rights organizations. It focuses on advocating for the release of political prisoners, ending torture, and abolishing the death penalty. Amnesty's global campaigns have drawn attention to human rights abuses in countries around the world, pressuring governments to take action and adopt reforms. Its research and reporting have provided crucial evidence for international advocacy and policymaking.

Direct Support and Humanitarian Assistance

In addition to advocacy, NGOs provide direct support to individuals and communities affected by human rights violations. This support can take various forms, including legal assistance, medical care, psychosocial support, and the provision of essential services in conflict or disaster areas.

Médecins Sans Frontières (Doctors Without Borders)

Médecins Sans Frontières (MSF) provides medical assistance to people affected by conflict, epidemics, disasters, or exclusion from healthcare. MSF operates in over 70 countries, delivering emergency medical care and highlighting the plight of those in need. The organization's work goes beyond medical care; it also advocates for global health issues, such as access to essential medicines and vaccines, highlighting the intersection of human rights and health.

Monitoring and Reporting

NGOs are vital in monitoring human rights situations, documenting abuses, and holding perpetrators accountable. They conduct on-the-ground investigations, gather evidence, and publish reports that bring attention to violations. This documentation is essential for building cases for international intervention, legal action, and policy changes.

Human Rights Watch

Human Rights Watch conducts research and advocacy on human rights violations worldwide. Its reports provide detailed documentation of abuses, including war crimes, torture, and political repression. By shining a light on violations, Human Rights Watch plays a key role in pressuring governments and international bodies to take action. Its findings are often cited in international forums and contribute to shaping human rights discourse and policy.

Legal Advocacy and Strategic Litigation

NGOs engage in legal advocacy and strategic litigation to challenge unjust laws, seek redress for victims, and promote human rights standards. This includes filing cases in national courts, regional human rights courts, and international tribunals, as well as providing legal representation and support to individuals and communities.

The Centre for Constitutional Rights (CCR)

The Centre for Constitutional Rights is a US-based NGO that uses legal action to advance civil rights and social justice. CCR has been involved in landmark cases challenging government policies on issues such as torture, indefinite detention, and racial profiling. Through strategic litigation, CCR has sought to set legal precedents and promote systemic change in the protection of human rights.

International Intervention

International intervention in human rights crises involves a range of actions, from diplomatic pressure and economic sanctions to military intervention and peacekeeping operations. The effectiveness and ethical implications of such interventions are often debated, as they involve complex considerations of sovereignty, justice, and the protection of human life. This section examines case studies of international intervention, highlighting the challenges and outcomes of these efforts.

Rwanda Genocide (1994)

Background: In 1994, Rwanda experienced one of the most horrific genocides of the 20th century, in which an estimated 800,000 Tutsi and moderate Hutu were systematically slaughtered by Hutu extremists over a period of 100 days. The genocide was fueled by long-standing ethnic tensions, political instability, and the failure of international actors to intervene in a timely manner.

International Response

UN Peacekeeping: The United Nations Assistance Mission for Rwanda (UNAMIR) was initially deployed to facilitate a peace agreement between the Hutu-led government and the Tutsi-led Rwandan Patriotic Front (RPF). However, UNAMIR was ill-equipped and lacked the mandate to intervene effectively when the genocide began. Despite warnings from UN officials on the ground, the international community failed to authorize a robust intervention to stop the mass killings.

Post-Genocide Intervention

After the genocide, the international community provided humanitarian assistance and support for Rwanda's recovery and reconciliation efforts. The establishment of the International Criminal Tribunal for Rwanda (ICTR) in 1994 aimed to prosecute those responsible for the genocide and deliver justice. The ICTR indicted and prosecuted key figures involved in orchestrating the genocide, contributing to the development of international criminal law.

Lessons Learned

The international community's failure to prevent and halt the Rwandan genocide has been widely regarded as a profound moral and operational failure. It highlighted the limitations of UN peacekeeping mandates, the challenges of mobilizing timely international action, and the need for a more effective mechanism to prevent mass atrocities. The genocide prompted a re-evaluation of international norms and practices, leading to the development of the 'Responsibility to Protect' (R2P) doctrine, which asserts that states have a responsibility to protect their populations from genocide, war crimes, ethnic cleansing, and crimes against humanity and that the international community has a role in assisting and, if necessary, intervening when states fail to do so.

Kosovo Conflict (1998-99)

Background: The Kosovo conflict was marked by violent repression by the Yugoslav government under Slobodan Milošević against the ethnic Albanian population of Kosovo. The conflict escalated into a humanitarian crisis, with widespread reports of ethnic cleansing, massacres, and mass displacement of civilians.

International Response

NATO Intervention: In response to the humanitarian crisis and the failure of diplomatic efforts to resolve the conflict, the North Atlantic Treaty Organization (NATO) launched a military intervention in March 1999. NATO's air campaign targeted Yugoslav military infrastructure to halt the atrocities and force the withdrawal of Yugoslav forces from Kosovo. The intervention, conducted without explicit UN Security Council authorization, was controversial but ultimately led to the withdrawal of Yugoslav forces and the establishment of a UN-administered protectorate in Kosovo.

UN Administration and Peacebuilding

Following the conflict, the United Nations Interim Administration Mission in Kosovo (UNMIK) was established to administer the territory, maintain security, and facilitate the development of democratic institutions. Kosovo declared independence in 2008, although its status remains disputed by some countries.

Lessons Learned: The Kosovo intervention was a pivotal moment in the evolution of humanitarian intervention and the debate over state sovereignty versus human rights. While the NATO intervention succeeded in preventing further atrocities, it raised questions about the legality and legitimacy of military intervention without UN Security Council approval. The Kosovo case underscored the need for a clear international framework for humanitarian intervention and the importance of post-conflict reconstruction and peacebuilding.

Syria Conflict (2011-Present)

Background: The Syrian conflict began in 2011 as a popular uprising against the regime of President Bashar al-Assad, but it quickly devolved into a brutal civil war involving multiple actors, including the Syrian government, various rebel groups, and international powers. The conflict has been marked by widespread human rights abuses, including the use of chemical weapons, indiscriminate bombings, torture, and mass displacement of civilians.

International Response UN and Diplomatic Efforts: The United Nations has engaged in diplomatic efforts to broker a peace settlement, including the Geneva peace talks and the appointment of special envoys to facilitate negotiations. However, these efforts have been hindered by the intransigence of the parties involved and the complex geopolitical interests at play.

Humanitarian Assistance and Sanctions: The UN and international NGOs have provided humanitarian assistance to millions of Syrians affected by the conflict, including refugees and internally displaced persons. The international community has also imposed sanctions on the Syrian government in an attempt to pressure it to cease hostilities and engage in negotiations.

Limited Military Intervention: In response to the use of chemical weapons by the Syrian government, United States, United Kingdom, and France have conducted limited military strikes against Syrian military targets. However, there has been no comprehensive international military intervention, largely due to divisions within the UN Security Council and concerns about the potential for further escalation.

Lessons Learned: The Syrian conflict represents one of the most challenging humanitarian crises of the 21st century and highlights the limitations of international intervention. The inability of the international community to achieve a peaceful resolution or provide adequate protection for civilians has been widely criticized. The conflict has exposed the limitations of the existing international system in addressing mass atrocities and the need for more effective mechanisms for conflict prevention, resolution, and accountability.

The role of international organizations in promoting and protecting human rights is complex and multifaceted. The United Nations, through its various bodies and mechanisms, has established a global framework for human rights, setting standards and providing mechanisms for accountability. NGOs have played a crucial role in advocating for human rights, providing support to victims, and holding governments accountable.

However, the effectiveness of international intervention in human rights crises is often limited by political considerations, questions of sovereignty, and the complexities of each situation. The case studies of Rwanda, Kosovo, and Syria illustrate the challenges and dilemmas of international intervention, including the need for timely and decisive action, the importance of post-conflict reconstruction, and the ongoing struggle to balance respect for state sovereignty with the imperative to protect human rights.

As the world continues to grapple with human rights challenges, the role of international organizations and NGOs remains vital. Their efforts to promote universal human rights, advocate for the marginalized, and intervene in times of crisis are essential to building a more just and humane global society. Yet, the pursuit of human rights is an ongoing struggle, requiring continuous commitment, innovation, and collaboration to address the evolving challenges of our time.

About the Author

Dr Ajaypal Kalyan brings a unique blend of personal experience, deep philosophical insight, and a passion for exploring the human condition. With a keen eye for detail and a talent for weaving together anecdotes, literary references, and cinematic moments, he creates a rich tapestry that invites readers to embark on a unique journey of self-discovery and growth.

His work is a testament to the power of introspection, authenticity, and the relentless pursuit of understanding life's profound mysteries.

About the Author

[illegible] exploring the human condition. With a keen eye for detail and a talent for weaving together anecdotes, literary references, and cinematic moments, he creates a rich tapestry that invites readers to embark on a unique journey of self-discovery and growth.

His work is a testament to the power of introspection, authenticity, and the relentless pursuit of understanding life's profound mysteries.

International Intervention

International interventions in human rights crises involves a range of actions, from diplomatic pressure and economic sanctions to military intervention and peacekeeping operations. The effectiveness and ethical implications of such interventions are often debated, as they involve complex considerations of sovereignty, justice, and the protection of human life. This [illegible] of international intervention, highlighting the challenges and outcomes of these efforts.

Rwandan Genocide (1994)

Background: In 1994, Rwanda experienced one of the most horrific genocides of the 20th century, in which an estimated 800,000 Tutsi and moderate Hutu were systematically slaughtered by Hutu extremists over a period of 100 days. The genocide was fueled by long-standing ethnic tensions, political instability, and the failure of international actors to intervene effectively and timely.

International Response

UN Peacekeeping: The United Nations Assistance Mission for Rwanda (UNAMIR) was initially deployed to monitor a peace agreement between the Hutu-led government and the Tutsi-led Rwandan Patriotic Front (RPF). However, UNAMIR was ill-equipped and lacked the mandate to intervene effectively when the genocide began. Despite warnings from UN officials on the ground, the international community failed to authorize a robust intervention to stop the killing.